NOVEL SHORTCUTS

TEN TECHNIQUES That Ensure A Great First Draft

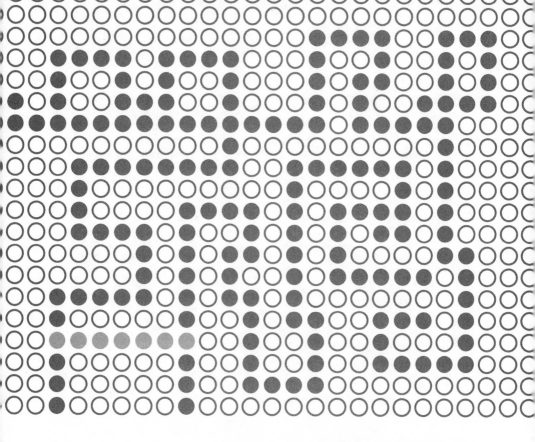

NOVEL SHORTCUTS

TEN TECHNIQUES That Ensure A Great First Draft

LAURA WHITCOMB

WRITER'S DIGEST BOOKS
Cincinnati, Ohio
www.writersdigest.com

For more resources for writers, visit www.writersdigest.com/books.

To receive a free weekly e-mail newsletter delivering tips and updates about writing and about Writer's Digest products, register directly at http://news letters.fwpublications.com.

13 12 11 10 09   5 4 3 2 1

Distributed in Canada by Fraser Direct
100 Armstrong Avenue
Georgetown, Ontario, Canada L7G 5S4
Tel: (905) 877-4411

Distributed in the U.K. and Europe by David & Charles
Brunel House, Newton Abbot, Devon, TQ12 4PU, England
Tel: (+44) 1626-323200, Fax: (+44) 1626-323319
E-mail: postmaster@davidandcharles.co.uk

Distributed in Australia by Capricorn Link
P.O. Box 704, Windsor, NSW 2756 Australia
Tel: (02) 4577-3555

Library of Congress Cataloging-in-Publication Data
Whitcomb, Laura.
   Novel shortcuts : ten techniques that ensure a great first draft / Laura Whitcomb. -- 1st ed.
      p. cm.
   Includes index.
   ISBN 978-1-58297-567-2 (pbk. : alk. paper)
   I. Title.
   PN3365.W48 2009
   808.3--dc22   2008044221

Edited by Kelly Nickell
Designed by Terri Woesner
Production coordinated by Mark Griffin

DEDICATION

For my grandmother, Ruby, a poet and a storyteller who would drape a quilt over my lap and
read me fairy tales. And to my future child for
whom I plan to do the same.

ACKNOWLEDGMENTS

Thanks to my sister, Cynthia, for being my first editor; my agent, Ann Rittenberg, for her unfailing friendship and splendid agenting; my editor, Kelly Nickell, for her support and excellent guidance; my dog, Maximus, for being patient in the face of long writing days; and to the writers and teachers who let me gather inspiration from their hearts and souls.

TABLE OF CONTENTS

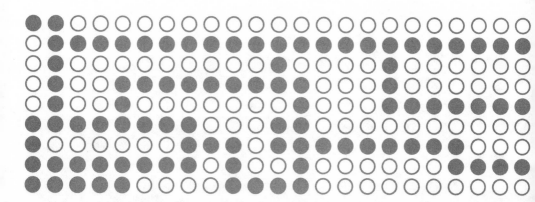

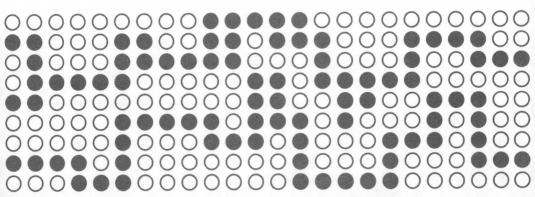

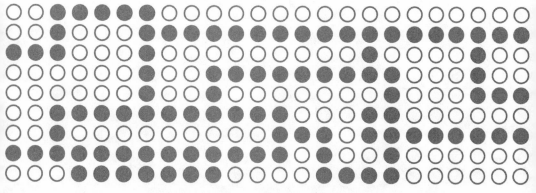

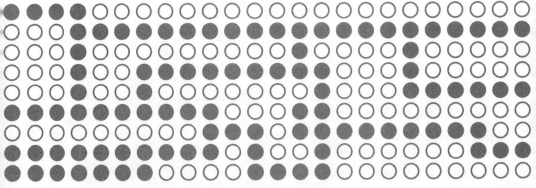

INTRODUCTION

I was one of those overnight successes that was twenty years in the making. When my literary agent, Ann Rittenberg, sold my first novel, *A Certain Slant of Light*, to Houghton Mifflin, I had been practicing my craft for more than two decades. I believe this was one of the reasons that Ann chose me to co-author *Your First Novel* with her for Writer's Digest Books. She liked my ideas and appreciated the hard work I'd put into preparing as a writer. In *YFN* I started from the beginning—everything from latching onto an idea to refining metaphors, all the methods and tricks that had helped me break in.

When my second novel sold on a synopsis and sample, I was facing my first deadline on the creation phase of fiction writing. I knew how to write fast. I'd had years of practice in getting a mediocre draft down in as little as one weekend, but that was a draft I could hide away for months of revision. And I knew how to write well. I love the rewriting process and knew what a great final draft felt like with *A Certain Slant of Light*. What I was facing now was a limited number of weeks before my beloved publishers would be holding my new manuscript in their hands and be either inspired or disappointed.

What I needed was a fast way to jump to that higher-quality draft. I couldn't wait for the power, magic, and beauty that usually came with a third or fifth draft. I needed it all now. So I started trying everything I could think of in an attempt to get at my personal greatness in less time. I discovered some new techniques and reworked some old ones, my take on speed depth in fiction writing. When I was a beginner I may have been embarrassed about some of my peculiar writing techniques, but now I feel bold and want to tell the truth about how I write. I used to think I was such a weirdo that hardly anyone would be able to relate to most of my creative writing habits, but the more writers I meet, the more I realize that most of us writers are weirdos. And if something works for me, it may work for you, too.

CHAPTER 1

FINDING THE CORE OF YOUR NOVEL

Books are uniquely portable magic.
—Stephen King

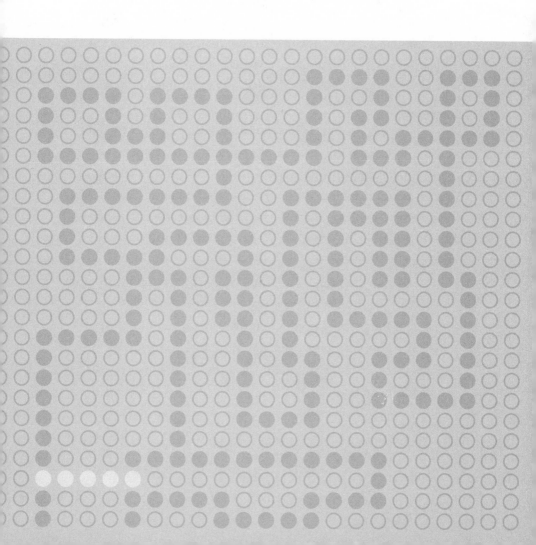

Whether you are at the outlining stage of your novel or you have finished the rough draft, or even a tenth draft, the exercises in this book can help you write faster and better. I wish I had thought of them all before I started my second novel. (It would have made life easier, for instance, if I had developed the "Shortcut to the Scene" exercise [see chapter four] in the planning stages instead of halfway through the draft.) But you can use these techniques anytime.

At the beginning of each chapter I will explain how the shortcut provided helped me increase my speed and raised my writing to a higher level. From using storytelling device props and drafting subplot charts to creating a soundtrack for your novel and using magic visualization—I've tried to think of everything that might make your writing shine brighter in less time.

Through using the shortcut in this first chapter you will find (or rediscover) the core of your story, the first and most essential step to writing a great novel. A common reason that new writers quit writing a novel is because they can't remember why they thought it was such a good idea in the first place. *Why did I choose this story? What got me all fired up? Where did that excitement go?*

In this chapter I'll talk about getting at the most significant idea in your story, clarifying the who, where, and what of the premise, and strengthening the drive of the plot. I'll also give you some exercises for reminding you why you have no choice but to write the wonderful novel you are meant to write.

Recommended Reading

- *Zen in the Art of Writing* by Ray Bradbury: Inspiration on the wonder of storytelling.

- *On Writing* by Stephen King: Inspiration on the writing life.

- *The Writer's Digest Handbook of Novel Writing*: "The Question at the Core of Your Story" by Ronald B. Tobias.

WHY THIS STORY?

When you decided to write your novel, there was a reason. It might have been because you liked the idea of being a novelist, or it might have been because you were already a published novelist and your editor was expecting a draft by the end of the year, but more likely there was something about the idea for your novel that drove you to choose it.

In the Learning Channel documentary *The Seven Wonders of the World*, narrator John Romer explains why certain statues and structures were chosen as historic icons. He stands at the top of the Golden Gate Bridge and tells us that the landmark below is not the tallest or the longest or the oldest or the most beautiful of its kind, but that it doesn't matter because, "it's all about *wonder*."

It's the same with writing. A story doesn't have to address a subject that has never been touched on before. It doesn't need to win a Pulitzer Prize or be a thousand pages long or encompass twenty years of research. Storytelling is about wonder.

Sometimes as a writer you are haunted by a character who lingers in your imagination and won't leave you alone, or you dream about a place you've never been or a place where you grew up. Sometimes you are plagued by a scene that plays in your mind over and over like a movie and won't stop until you write it down. These aren't tricks of the mind, but of the heart and spirit. You don't decide to write a certain story so much as you are called to write it. Your story haunts you until you have no other choice. It courts you. It dazzles you. You conjured this idea from your soul. It's all about wonder.

To realize your idea and get it down on paper faster and with greater depth, you need to understand the power that drew you to it, pull that glowing core out, and look at it closely. Something about it appeals to you so much that you'd be willing to spend months creating it. Tapping into the core of your novel helps you write the story faster and better because, when you tune into the potential for greatness in your novel, you feel more energized about writing it. You're infatuated with it. You don't fear it will be a waste of time. Every page introduces your readers to this great story you've come up with. All the scenes are infused with that excitement. You write it faster because you can't wait to get to the height of the story. You write it well because you feel the wonder in it—the wonder that comes from your heart out onto the page.

What is at the core of your story? Who is the character at the center of this book? When you go into your story, where are you in time and space? When you get there, what creates the emotion? What's the turmoil at hand? If you are already clear about this, great. Because how quickly, and how well, you are able to write your novel depends on your recognizing these elements as irresistible.

CLARIFYING THE PREMISE

The premise is a statement that briefly describes your story. It covers the main issue, the problem that arcs across the entire novel. For me, a good premise also needs to state whom the story is about and where the story takes place. The theme of a great story, the idea of what the story is really about, can present itself in a well-constructed premise simply because the who, where, and what's wrong of the story are clearly defined. For many writers it's important to know the premise before they start writing because it will act as a light shining on the path before them. It's easy to stumble off into an irrelevant subplot or lose track of a character arc if you are blindly feeling your way from page to page. When you have a strong premise in place, the throughline of your novel will help guide you. The premise should be short and catchy. Don't go into detail. As readers, we want to become one with the main character, so just tell us who we are, where we are, and what the problem is. First we'll break down the three elements.

Who Are We?

Who is your main character? You may say you have two main characters or twenty, but it should still be mainly one person's story. Focusing on a central character strengthens the narrative. If you skip about and give the same attention to a dozen characters, readers will feel lost and confused. If you can't pin down the main character to one person (or two in a love story like *Romeo and Juliet*), if you still think your book is equally about six main characters, then consider your favorite novel. Whose story is it? With some books it's an easy call. Margaret Mitchell's *Gone with the Wind* is Scarlett's story, Louisa May Alcott's *Little Women* is Jo's, Mary Stewart's *The Crystal Cave* is Merlin's, and J.D. Salinger's *The Catcher in the Rye* is Holden's story. The other characters in these stories are absolutely important and necessary, but they aren't the main character.

With some stories that center on relationships there might be some debate. *The Princess Bride* by William Goldman: Buttercup or Westley? *A Separate Peace* by John Knowles: Gene or Finny? *The Green Mile* by Stephen King: Paul Edgecombe or is it really John Coffey? It's vital that in *The Dead Zone* by Stephen King we get inside the heads of both the villain and the hero, but come on, we all know it's Johnny's story. Novels that include several central characters and still succeed, such as *Ragtime* by E.L. Doctorow, work because the authors are careful to flesh out each person and interweave their storylines. But when Doctorow came up with the idea, he *probably* had a gut instinct as to the key character. Okay, I confess, pinpointing the "who" in novels is subjective, but what's important is that you feel who the central character is in your own novel and focus on him first.

Some genres tend to dictate a main character—mysteries often have the detective as the central character, and romance novels are usually focused on a female protagonist. Some narrative choices make the choice for you—most first-person narrators are the main character in the story. But don't feel bound by statistics or convention. If you want to write a murder mystery where the detective is a minor character and the dead man's landlord is the hero or a love story told from the point of view of the woman's pet ferret, more power to you. Your genre, plot, point of view, theme—nothing should force a central character decision on you.

Your gut knows whose story you will be telling with your novel. You don't need to make that character a first-person narrator or follow her around in limited third-person. You can tell the story with an omniscient voice if you want to. But knowing whom the story is *really* about will help you focus the book.

When you know whose story you are telling, when you picture her as the star of the book, you'll be able to see her more clearly and accurately. You'll hear her voice, even if she doesn't act as narrator. You'll know what she would say and how she would say it in dialogue or in her thoughts. You'll be able to more easily track her desires and fears; you'll know what kinds of conflicts to throw at her to increase tension and raise the stakes. Her backstory will become clearer in your mind, and her emotions will begin to color the story and enhance your themes. You can certainly write your other characters in just as fine detail and have as many characters as you can juggle, but you need a grounding character.

And if that's not enough, remember this: Books with strong characters driving them get more attention from agents and editors, and eventually critics and book buyers, because a strong central character makes it faster and easier for the readers to bond with the story.

Where Are We?

Next, you need to choose a setting. Your story may have several, and they may each be as magnificent as the next, but choose one central setting, and when you do, place it in history as well. It's vital that you love where your novel takes place geographically and historically because you have to be able to make the truth and beauty of that setting come to life in your readers' head in order for your novel to shine. You need to be able to decorate your prose with not only the accurate descriptions of the setting physically, but with the attitudes, philosophies, and quirks of the place and time. The setting is like a supporting character. It has dreams and flaws and gifts, just like your hero and your villain.

Some examples of "where" include:

- *I, Claudius* by Robert Graves: first century A.D. Roman palace

- *The Name of the Rose* by Umberto Eco: fourteenth century, Italian monastery

- *The Hound of the Baskervilles* by Arthur Conan Doyle: Victorian era, house at edge of an English moor

- *The Adventures of Huckleberry Finn* by Mark Twain: nineteenth century, raft on the Mississippi River

- *To Kill a Mockingbird* by Harper Lee: 1930s, courtroom in a small southern town

- *Cujo* by Stephen King: 1980s, the inside of a parked car

If the above stories were separated from their settings they would cease to exist: Claudius is an actual historical character bound to his own time and place. *The Name of the Rose* must take place in the period and area where the Holy Inquisition ruled. In *The Hound of the Baskervilles*, the killer beast needed the moors to hide in. The story would have fallen apart if the characters had been able to ring each other up on cell phones. In *The Adventures of Huckleberry Finn*, the period of history was vital to Jim's need to escape in search of freedom, and the river was such an essential character in the novel that it would be impossible to imagine the story without it. *Cujo* would never have worked if the characters were safe in a house with a phone and a shotgun instead of trapped in a car. Your setting needs to be so tightly bound with your story that they become inseparable.

As with your central character, when you know your story's setting, when you picture the details and quality of light, when you can smell it and walk it, measuring the length of the place with your strides, when you hear its bird cries or siren calls, you'll be able to more easily write your characters' reactions to that environment. You'll know their relationships with the room or meadow or office or ship. You'll know what kinds of comforts or hazards it has in store and how it relates to your themes. You'll be able to write the story faster and with greater depth because the setting will be second nature to you, and it will drive your characters and story problems onward.

What's Wrong?

Now you need to clarify the problem. A novel's central problem should to be something that can't be easily righted and is serious enough to sustain the entire story. Being thirsty is not a problem if you can pick up the glass of water in front of you and drink. You have to make sure the problem is real. And don't confuse a problem with a character's drive or goal. They're connected, but they are *not* the same thing. *Scarlett wants Ashley* is a goal. *Scarlett wants Ashley, but he's happily married* is a problem. A character's goal is only a problem if something is blocking her success.

Here are some examples of central problems in well-known novels:

- *The Member of the Wedding* by Carson McCullers: Frankie longs to belong somewhere but is shut out of everything from the clique of her former playmates to her brother's honeymoon.

- *The Da Vinci Code* by Dan Brown: Langdon struggles to uncover a mystery, but the clues are veiled and he's been framed for murder.

- *Othello* by William Shakespeare: Othello doesn't want to believe his wife is unfaithful, but he's being lied to and tricked by his best friend.

- *Rebecca* by Daphne du Maurier: Newlyweds' bliss is blocked by the groom's apparent attachment to his dead wife.

The Problem Checklist

When you are in the outline stage of your novel, it's good to make sure you build a worthy central problem. But if you're in the middle of the draft and the story feels weak or off balance, don't worry. It's not too late to make adjustments. Double-check the following list to make sure your problem is causing enough trouble.

• **Make your problem serious.** Your protagonist needs something badly that he does not have and may never get, but that he would do anything (or almost anything) to possess. *He is dying of thirst in the desert and must find water or die.* Or your protagonist is afraid something specific will happen and she is struggling to stop it. *She is doing everything she can to keep the ship she is on afloat, but nothing is working and she is afraid she will drown.*

• **Make sure the problem doesn't have a logical solution that your character is ignoring.** What you want to avoid is your readers saying, "Why doesn't he just _____ ?" If there's a way out of the problem that your character is being too stupid to clue into, it will ruin your story. If your character needs to find her long-lost brother and could simply google his name and age, if your character is trapped in an unhappy relationship and all she has to do is get in her car and drive away, if your character is estranged from her parents and all she has to do is walk up to their door and say *I'm sorry* or *I love you*, the readers are going to be frustrated and bored when the character continues to be blind to that obvious solution. Make sure your character has no idea of her brother's name or the city in which he lives. Make sure she can't leave her boyfriend because she loves his children and has no claim to custody. Make sure your character's parents will not speak to her or that they sue her, have her committed, or try to murder her. Something big must stand in the way and make that first obvious solution impossible.

• **Make sure your problem can be stretched over a whole manuscript.** Your problem can't just be serious; it has to be big enough to sustain an entire novel. In *Gone with the Wind*, the problem wasn't that Scarlett needed a beautiful dress and was too poor to afford one. Or that she wanted to be wealthy like she was before the war but now had only turnips to eat. Those were problems that could be solved in one scene or a couple of chapters. There had to be a grand problem that would start in chapter one and not be solved until the last chapter. This is why Scarlett's obsession with Ashley has to continue through everything from the breakout of civil war to the breakdown of her marriage.

• **Make sure your problem fits your character.** A whole novel can run on the "Scarlett still loves Ashley" problem only because Scarlett is self-centered and stubborn. If another kind of woman, a selfless, good girl, had been in love with Ashley, she might have suffered a broken heart silently, gone off to be a brilliant Civil War nurse, married a sweet man whom she liked and respected, had ten children, and lived happily (if dully) ever after. Make sure the problem you give your protagonist is something that would consume your character.

• **Make sure your subplots are connected to your problem.** Your plot will also include several other problems, other fears and desires for your characters to deal with, but there needs to be a main problem, one that takes center stage, to hook your audience and keep the readers focused on the outcome, hungry for answers, victory, and relief. But this central problem needs to affect all the characters and their subplots. Scarlett's desire for Ashley tied into her relationship with Rhett, her rescue of Mellie and her baby, her marriage to Mellie's brother, her choices as a businesswoman, everything. Main problems should ignite smaller problems throughout your subplots. If a subplot is completely untouched by your central problem, that subplot needs to be rewritten or removed from the book.

Beefing Up Your Problem

If you find that your central plot problem is weak, see if one of the following tips might help make it more dramatic.

> **1. Add an additional obstacle.** If the problem is that your hero needs to find a hidden bomb, give her a broken arm or a memory lapse, or have her support system snatched away from her.

2. **Raise the stakes.** If a career will be destroyed by the outcome of a lawsuit, throw in something else like the destruction of a marriage, visitation rights, or an inheritance.

3. **Make the protagonist more emotionally vulnerable about the situation.** If your hero is trying to keep a young woman from taking her own life, perhaps he lost a patient or a friend to suicide or survived a suicide attempt himself.

4. **Give your antagonist a boost.** If the problem is the solving of a code, make your villain an expert cryptologist. A murder trial? Make your villain the highest-paid defense attorney (or prosecutor) with the best record in town. Beef up the antagonist to make your protagonist the underdog.

5. **Provide the situation with a ticking clock.** If your problem is that an antidote needs to be discovered for a new poison, make sure someone important will die in X number of days if the hero fails. If a message must get through to army headquarters so an ambush can be avoided, make sure the readers know exactly how many hours until the troops are placed in harm's way.

When you know what the main problem is, when you feel that passion and struggle, turning the possible solutions over in your mind like your main character would, when you dwell on that fear or desire and realize how it relates to the backstory, characterization, and theme, the writing will go faster and will have more impact.

These three parts of the premise—the main character, the primary setting, and the central problem—are what storytelling is made of. The protagonist wouldn't be who he is if it weren't for the setting. The problem wouldn't be a problem if it weren't for the effect it has on the protagonist. The setting is where the problem is born.

Consider how the setting affects the other aspects of the premise. Romeo and Juliet would have lived happily ever after if they hadn't lived in a place where equally powerful families feuded openly and in a time when fathers chose their daughters' grooms. The setting gave birth to the problem and helped form the characters as well. The passionate longing felt by the lovers came from their love being forbidden.

How about the central character? The setting of a mental hospital would not have been a hostile environment if the protagonist in Ken Kesey's *One Flew Over the Cuckoo's Nest* had been a docile follower. There would have been no central problem.

The big problem must be tied to the setting and main character. It's the need to destroy an evil ring that makes Frodo a hero and makes the road he travels dangerous. No matter how clever or charming a sleuth might be, and no matter how shadowy the village churchyard, there's no cozy mystery without the dead body. The maiden voyage of the *Titanic* is not a story at all without the iceberg. It's that hunk of ice that brings out the best and worst in the characters involved and that turns a gorgeous, glowing oceanliner into a nightmare.

Knowing the main thrust of your idea, which includes these three interrelated parts of the premise, will help you focus on the most essential thread in your storyline. You'll waste less time going off on tangents if you feel grounded in your premise.

If you can write one paragraph explaining who your novel is about, where and when it takes place, and what the central problem is, as you would if you were composing a query letter for your story, you will throw out less paper as you write your first draft. Let's practice by making one-liners out of some who/where/whats:

- *A Certain Slant of Light* by Laura Whitcomb: Helen, who has been dead for over a century (there's your who), possesses a high school girl (implies the where is a twenty-first-century high school setting) so she can be with James, the ghost she has fallen in love with, but soon the lovers find they must unravel the pain of their hauntings, and that of the families with whom they are trapped, so they can return the bodies they have stolen (and here lies the problem).

- *A Morbid Taste for Bones* by Ellis Peters: Brother Cadfael, head of the twelfth-century Shrewsbury Abbey (the who and when), arrives in a remote Welsh village (where) to remove the remains of St. Winifred and finds himself in the middle of a murder mystery that brings with it scandal and possible ruin (the problem).

- *The Other Boleyn Girl* by Philippa Gregory: Mary (who), lover of Henry VIII (where and when), is replaced as the king's favorite by her scheming sister, Anne (the problem).

When a Good Premise Goes Bad

Sometimes a premise that seems like a great idea at first turns out to be a dud. And sometimes a great premise falls victim to poor execution. Here are the warning signs to look for in each case and tips that might help.

You Know Your Premise Is a Dud When ...

1. Your character wimps out. You have things happen to the main character instead of having him take action and take care of things himself. This happens when your main character was actually a bad fit for the setting and problem. As you started to write you probably found that the protagonist was either too weak to drive the action, held the wrong set of skills, or was constantly changing personalities. You tried to make him the hero, but it was just not working.

Tip: Either give your hero a galvanizing characteristic that makes him more dynamic (an unresolved mystery in his past, a phobia, a squelched desire for vengeance that is building up inside him) or choose someone else in the story, someone whose wants and needs are irreversibly tied to the setting and the outcome of the problem, to be your new central character. Another technique for making your character less wimpy is to give him a different job. My sister once solved a story problem by simply taking her protagonist out of an office cubical and making him a landscaper. (This is good for making your settings more interesting, too.)

2. Your setting bores you or feels forced. It seemed like a good idea at first, but now the setting is throwing the whole story off. This happens when you choose a setting without thinking it through. It made a nice picture in your head, but now you want to throw out the whole manuscript.

Tip: In your head, put your main character and your plot problem on a blank canvas. No setting at all. Do either the protagonist or the problem dictate a time in history? If so, look at that time and go through a list of places your story might take place: It must be the Great Depression, for instance, but could it happen in a hospital, an orphanage, a church, a college campus, a library, a beauty shop, a bank, a graveyard? Choose a new setting, one that adds tension by contrasting with the story or by mirroring the story. For example, a story about a child who wants to become an opera singer could have a setting that mirrors it—an opera house, a vaudeville theater, a piano store—or a contrasting setting—the hush of a library, a farm miles from any audience, an abbey peopled with nuns who have taken a vow of silence. If you aren't tied to a certain period of history, think about what year would offer the most tension to your plot. If you have a female protagonist who is a struggling writer, would it help if she lived in a time, for example, the Renaissance, when women were not expected to write? If your protagonist is a masonry artist, perhaps it would be more interesting if he lived in the twenty-first century when almost no cathedrals or castles are being built. Keep brainstorming until you feel comfortable with your new choice. Then try starting again with this new physical or historical environment that will be equipped to stimulate the story.

3. The problem gets solved too quickly. This happens when your characters, and the time and place they inhabit, are more powerful than the troubles you offered them. They're too smart, they have too many connections, they are good fighters and need to be. It's your problem that needs to be messier.

Tip: Throw a related obstacle in whenever you can. All the hero has to do is stop his true love from placing their newborn baby for adoption? It can't just be that he is estranged from the baby's mother or that the hospital is far away. You have to block him at every turn. No car. No bus fare. She won't take his calls. He loses his money. He hitches a ride and misses getting back in the car at the truck stop, and he left the address of the hospital in the car. He gets in a fight with the security guard in the hospital lobby and is arrested. Whatever you can do. The problem should be nearly insurmountable. Believe me, with ever-increasing difficulties, the story will work better and be more fun to write.

You'll Know You Are Failing Your Good Premise When ...

1. Your main character is coming off as flat. When you give your manuscript to family or friends for feedback, is your hero not coming across for them? This is confusing because in your head you know this character is a real winner. This happens when the idea of the character is fantastic, but for whatever reason you have underwritten her. Your readers can only experience what's on the page. If you've skimmed over the character's personality, your readers won't be able to latch onto her.

Tip: Go back and highlight every line in your manuscript so far where you describe your protagonist's words, actions, appearance, thoughts, or feelings. Now tweak all of those points, enhancing them with words that are character specific and that emphasize what is appealing or unique about her. Even if she's an antihero, what is it about her that would engage readers? Her obsession with even numbers? Her protective attitude toward animals? Her stutter? Let the readers in for a closer look at what you love about this person.

2. The setting is invisible. This happens when the setting is a perfect choice, but you have not taken the time to paint it in with a fine enough hand. The effect is usually that the readers are underwhelmed by the writing and are not sure why.

Tip: Take a few minutes and make a list of research that might help you make this setting or period in time come to life. Then, take a day to steep yourself in your setting. If you are still feeling a little detached from its color and vividness, write for ten minutes on your setting before you start work on the book each day.

3. The problem is unclear. This happens when you don't plan the unfolding of your main problem in enough detail. Even if your problem seems straightforward (your character has to escape from prison, save the town from a flood, or bring a sick friend to safety), how you unfold the idea for your readers, how you prepare them for each progressive stage of the problem, will make the difference between stirring their excitement and leaving them bewildered.

Tip: List ideas for each of these categories:

- Subtle details you could put near the beginning of your book to foreshadow problems your characters will have when solving the big problems.

- Ideas of complications that might make things trickier in the middle of your story.

- Last-minute hitches for your novel's climax. These should be things that will heighten the suspense and convince your readers that there's no way your hero can succeed.

Sometimes good ideas can be found in what you *aren't* thinking about. Once, while trying to think of new ideas for supernatural books, I started making a list down the left (the traditional) side of the page. But the ideas didn't feel right. So I moved my hand to the right side of the page and started a list called "Things I'm *Not* Thinking About," and under that heading, before I had time to realize this was a weird thing to do, I listed half a dozen other ideas, things I wasn't considering, and among these was an idea that panned out quite well. I'm not sure why it worked or if I could do it again, but if your well of inspiration feels dry and you want to think outside the box, try the right side of your page and the fresh side of your mind.

Fun Stuff

- Make a collage. Think about what you love in your novel while looking through old magazines and tear out pictures that make you happy and remind you of the core of wonder in your story. You can search for images on the Internet as well. Print out images that please you and stir your emotions, that inspire you to write that scene or description more beautifully. Then take a sheet of poster board and arrange the pictures you've gathered into a collage. Trim the clippings with scissors or by tearing so only the part of the image that you like appears. Glue the images down and hang the collage where you can see it from your writing area. When you look at these images, or even see them unconsciously in your peripheral vision, it will remind you how rich, interesting, and appealing your story truly is.

- Walk through a bookstore and look at book covers only. Get that glimpse of wonder hinting at what lies between the covers.

WRITING YOUR JACKET COPY AS REVELATION

After I had written the first draft of my second novel, *The Fetch*, and was in the midst of rewriting, my editor and I were asked to compose the book's jacket copy to run in the Houghton Mifflin catalog. The jacket copy that the author and editor put together consists of only the description of the story and a quoted passage pulled out of the novel.

The first version we wrote of *The Fetch* jacket copy seemed reasonable to us because we knew the story well, but one of the marketing people read it and said she didn't get it. I looked at the copy again and realized that it was not focusing on what was really important about the book. It emphasized the complex world of the Fetch, a community of death escorts who accompany souls from their bodies to Heaven, but I pictured the novel being more of a love story.

The Fetch jacket copy first draft:

> *"Are you an angel?" the actor asked, as so many others had before him.*
>
> *"I'm a Fetch," said Calder. "I'm your escort."*

> Although Calder died at nineteen, he's been a Fetch, escorting souls to Heaven, for over three hundred years. But then Calder does something he shouldn't—he steals the body of a holy man, Rasputin, amid the chaos of the Russian Revolution. In search of love, Calder sends Rasputin's soul into limbo,

misuses his power as a Fetch, and loses his sacred key.

But this is just the beginning. Calder's offense has repercussions that not even he can imagine, and soon innocent spirits are thrown into the darkness between life and the afterlife. On Earth, the living are plagued by hauntings, for the spirits of the ghost realm begin a revolution of their own.

Hunted by demons, Calder takes two royal children with him on his journey back to Heaven, children who had once been human but never will be again—a boy of thirteen, who has lost his chance to rule Russia, and a girl of seventeen, who will win Calder's heart.

I needed to transform the text so it sounded like a love story that just happened to be supernatural.

The Fetch jacket copy rewrite:

> *"There's something not right about you," said Ana. She wasn't teasing him. She was concerned about what she detected behind his eyes. This made Calder's skin tingle. "You're not telling me something."*
>
> *She was uncanny. Calder silently prayed she could not see how he had broken his Vows and upset her world and his own.*
>
> *"You're lonely," she told him. "It must be hard to pretend all the time."*

He felt a wave of sadness, sudden and deep.

"Don't be afraid," she told him. "Everyone has a secret. I'll keep yours."

Calder was a Fetch, a death escort, the first of his kind to step from Heaven back to Earth. The first to fall in love with a mortal girl. But when he climbed backward out of that Death Scene, into the chaos of the Russian Revolution, he tore a wound in the ghost realm where the spirits began a revolution of their own.

Then I looked at the new jacket copy and realized that it wasn't just those 150 words that needed tweaking. If I wanted to make sure the book was more about love than it was about magical rules, I needed to make sure the whole manuscript tilted in that direction. During the next rewrite of the book, my editor and I clarified and simplified the rules of the supernatural world I had created, which streamlined some of the complicated action. And we strengthened the love story, adding moments for the sweethearts in various scenes. Both of these changes made *The Fetch* a better book. I'm not sure these rewrite notes would have happened if the jacket copy hadn't made that flaw stand out. I wish I had written the jacket copy while I was still in the outline stage of *The Fetch*, but it never occurred to me. I would have saved time and the first draft would've come out better if I'd done this exercise and reminded myself that the story was a romance at its center.

Whether you have only an outline for your novel or a whole draft, the dust jacket exercise can sharpen your focus and bring potential faults to the surface where they can be identified and targeted. Your story will be improved, and you won't lose time on rewriting drafts.

As an example, let's pretend Anne Rice wrote an outline for *Interview with the Vampire* in which she alternated between the vampire Louis's tale and the interviewer's reaction to the story. The first draft of her jacket copy might have sounded like this:

> A young journalist faces his most unusual subject as he tapes an interview with a man who claims not to be a man at all, who claims to be dead yet not dead. For hours they stay hidden in a small hotel room as the journalist wonders if this creature to whom he listens will keep his promise and spare his life.

Let's pretend she looked at that copy and thought, "I don't want to hear the story of a reporter. I want to be the vampire." Here's the actual jacket text:

> Here are the confessions of a vampire, hypnotic, shocking, and chillingly erotic. This is a novel of mesmerizing beauty and astonishing force—a story of danger and flight, of love and loss, of suspense and resolution, and of the extraordinary power of the senses.

The real version focuses on the actual story told by the vampire. If Rice had had any trouble deciding on what or whom to focus (and I'm sure she did not), the dust jacket exercise would have given her the necessary clues to adjust the outline.

If you don't feel ready yet to start composing your jacket copy, warm up by reading the dust jacket on your favorite novel. If the text captures what made the book worthy of praise, *why* does it succeed? Is it apparent? Can you borrow any tricks?

Read the jackets of books you *haven't* read. Are those authors clear about their stories? Can you feel who the main character is in the book? Can you sense the location? Does the problem described on the dust jacket make you want to read the whole book?

Here are some examples of the jacket text from successful novels. See what you might glean from them to help you write your own.

Create a Strong Hook

San Francisco patron Bibi Chen has planned a journey of the senses along the famed Burma Road for eleven lucky friends. But after her mysterious death, Bibi watches aghast from her ghostly perch as the travelers veer off her itinerary and embark on a trail paved with cultural gaffes and tribal curses, Buddhist illusions and romantic desires. On

Christmas morning, the tourists cruise across
a misty lake and disappear.
> —*Saving Fish from Drowning*
> by Amy Tan

I like this jacket copy because it quickly introduces you to an appealing protagonist (a woman who plans a luscious vacation for her friends and is now a ghost—very original), a fascinating setting (Burma? Buddhist illusions? Fabulous), and, especially effective, a catchy problem (the entire party has disappeared—now there's a great hook). Try to grab your potential readers. Tell them just enough and no more.

Use Key Phrases

A hypnotically atmospheric story set in nineteenth-century London. When puritanical artist Henry Chester sees delicate child beauty Effie, he makes her his favorite model and, before long, his bride. But Henry, volatile and repressed, is in love with an ideal. Passive, docile, and asexual, the woman he projects onto Effie is far from the woman she really is. And when Effie begins to discover the murderous depths of Henry's hypocrisy, her latent passion will rise to the surface. *Sleep, Pale Sister* combines the ethereal beauty of a Pre-Raphaelite painting with a chilling high gothic tale ...
> —*Sleep, Pale Sister* by Joanne Harris

This jacket text could sound like a soap opera, but instead, the phrase "delicate child beauty" in juxtaposition with the later phrase "Pre-Raphaelite painting" gives the premise a literary eeriness that, for me anyway, made the book impossible not to buy and read. Could the tone of your book be illustrated with a key phrase or two?

Round Up Your Suspects

A serial murderer is terrorizing Seattle, hunting and scalping white men. And the crimes of the so-called Indian Killer have triggered a wave of violence and racial hatred. Seattle's Native Americans are shaken, none more so than John Smith. Born Indian, raised white, Smith desperately yearns for his lost heritage and seeks his elusive true identity. He meets Marie, a stormy Indian activist particularly outraged by people like Jack Wilson, the mystery writer who passes himself as part Indian. As a bigoted radio personality incites whites to seek revenge, tensions mount, Smith fights to slake the anger that engulfs him ... and the Indian Killer claims yet another life.
—*Indian Killer* by Sherman Alexie

This may not work for every murder mystery, but here the way four possible killers are introduced in only 107 words fascinated me, especially because their varied personalities make for a lot of interesting conflict. If you are writing a whodunit, try writing the suspects into your jacket copy.

Showcase the Protagonist's Voice

I don't talk much about those days. Never did. I don't know why—I worked on circuses for nearly seven years, and if that isn't fodder for conversation, I don't know what is.

Actually I do know why: I never trusted myself. I was afraid I'd let it slip. I knew how important it was to keep her secret, and keep it I did—for the rest of her life, and then beyond.

In seventy years, I've never told a blessed soul.

Though he may not speak of them, the memories still dwell inside Jacob Jankowski's ninety-something-year-old mind. Memories of himself as a young man, tossed by fate onto a rickety train that was home to the Benzini Brothers Most Spectacular Show on Earth. Memories of a world filled with freaks and clowns, with wonder and pain and anger and passion; a world with its own narrow, irrational rules, its own way of life, and its own way of death. The world of the circus: to Jacob it was both salvation and a living hell ...

—*Water for Elephants* by Sara Gruen

Jacob speaks to us for less than a hundred words, but we already feel like we know him. He makes confessions, whets our appetite for circus stories, and teases us with a secret. I wanted to know everything about him by the time I finished this jacket copy. (And the book does not disappoint.)

Show Off Your Literary Chops

Recalls the experiences of a young man in frontier Montana: of his minister father, who taught his sons the ways of grace and fly fishing; of his brother, an artist at trout fishing but less than successful at life; and the swift, cold rivers that run from the heart of the mountain into the still-mysterious heart of man.

—*A River Runs Through It*
by Norman Maclean

If you can manage to capture the beauty of your prose as concisely as this dust jacket demonstrates Maclean's voice, do it. If you can impress a potential book buyer in one paragraph, they'll have little choice but to read on.

If Your Plot Is Unique, Show It Off

Paul Iverson's life changes in an instant. He returns home one day to find that his wife, Lexy, has died under strange circumstances. The only witness was their dog, Lorelei, whose anguished barking brought help to the scene—but too late.

In the days and weeks that follow, Paul begins to notice strange "clues" in their home: books rearranged on their shelves, a mysterious phone call, and other suggestions that nothing about Lexy's last afternoon was quite what it seemed. Reeling from grief, Paul is determined to decipher this evidence and unlock the mystery of her death.

But he can't do it alone; he needs Lorelei's help. A linguist by training, Paul embarks on an impossible endeavor: a series of experiments designed to teach Lorelei to communicate what she knows. Perhaps behind her wise and earnest eyes lies the key to what really happened to the woman he loved …

—*The Dogs of Babel*
by Carolyn Parkhurst

I don't think this jacket text is fabulously written, but the extremely unusual plot is explained well enough to capture the readers' curiosity. I, for one, needed to know if Lorelei eventually found a way to speak to her grieving master. If your setting and characters sound ordinary but your plot is fascinating, emphasize it.

Add Shadows

What happens to us after we die? Chris Nielson had no idea, until an unexpected accident cut his life short, separating him abruptly from his beloved wife, Annie. Now Chris must discover the true nature of life after death.

But even Heaven is not complete without Annie, and when tragedy threatens to divide them forever, Chris risks his very soul to save Annie from an eternity of despair. Can love bring together what Heaven and Hell have torn asunder?

—*What Dreams May Come*
by Richard Matheson

If your story teeters on the edge of "too sentimental," make sure there's a dark spot. This premise could have sounded boringly sappy but for the idea that beloved Annie might be in Hell. If your premise is a little on the soft side, make sure the central problem in the story sounds threatening.

Add Light

Marc Seidman awakens to find himself in an ICU, hooked up to an IV, his head swathed in bandages. Twelve days earlier, he'd had an enviable life as a successful surgeon, living in a peaceful suburban neighborhood with his beautiful wife and a baby he adored. Now he lies in a hospital bed, shot by an unseen assailant. His wife has been killed, and his six-month-old daughter, Tara, has vanished. But

> just when his world seems forever shattered,
> something arrives to give Marc new hope: a
> ransom note.
>> —*No Second Chance*
>> by Harlan Coben

In contrast, this story sounds at first intolerably depressing until we get to the last few words and picture Marc being reunited with his baby girl. If your premise sounds too dark, give the readers a glimpse of hope.

More Tips for Writing Your Jacket Copy

• **Set up the big question.** You want to emphasize what makes the story compelling. First think, what is the most important event or change that takes place? A character falls in love, finds her way home, defeats a rival, gives up her child? Now think, what suspenseful situation will make your readers want to open the book? There is always a question or an implied question. Look at the dust jacket samples. A ransom note arrives—what does it say? Can love bring together Heaven and Hell? What were the circus world's narrow irrational rules about death? When they created the preview for the movie *Casablanca*, they didn't show Rick being noble at the airport, sacrificing his own happiness by sending his true love away to safety. They showed Rick in his club, seeing Ilsa for the first time on the arm of another man, with Nazis at the next table. Think of the most important element in your story and then think of the "what if" that came before. Set up your question in the dust jacket text, but leave the readers wanting more.

• **Make sure the jacket text reflects the tone of the book.** If your novel is a hard-boiled and clever mystery, be edgy and clever in your dust jacket text. If you're writing a poetic literary novel, make sure you sound like a poet. If your book is a comedic romp, make them laugh reading the back cover.

• **Don't use phrases that put people to sleep.** If you use a cliché in your dust jacket, you'll make people think you're derivative and pass you by. Your reporter protagonist shouldn't be hungry for a story. The lovers should never be star-crossed. The streets can't be mean. And don't just find a different way of wording the cliché—look for the differences in your story and use those as your descriptors. In Carolyn Parkhurst's novel, a widower doesn't seek comfort in the arms of another woman; he seeks it in the eyes of his dog.

Once you have a draft of the jacket text, you'll probably be able to tell if it's good. If it is good, you'll feel the joy of it when you read it back. If you don't love it, try again or put the exercise away for a while before you redo it. But once it's good, ask yourself these questions:

If you only have an outline of your novel so far, ask:

- Does it feel like my story will fulfill the promise made on the dust jacket?

- Do I need to change my outline because something inherent in the story is out of balance?

If you have a draft (or a partial draft) already down, ask:

- Does the jacket copy sound like my book?

- Do I need to tweak the manuscript to make it as good as the dust jacket?

A NOTE ABOUT TITLES

Walker Percy once said, "A good title should be like a good metaphor; it should intrigue without being too baffling or too obvious." Finding the right title can help your writing surge forward. It can flavor the story in a way that nudges you onto the right path for tone, voice, and theme. Remember that your title should appeal to the readers (you want them to pick up the book off the shelf and buy it), and it should fit the story, like a little illustration of the big picture. Think of titles of books you have loved. *To Kill a Mockingbird* is not just a touchstone from a morality lesson shared by a father and daughter; it's poetic imagery that perfectly fits the tone of the story.

A single word can also be a perfect title. *Rebecca* is just a woman's name, but the fact that it is not the protagonist's name, but that of her new groom's dead wife, tells you a lot about the story.

You can find ideas for titles everywhere from song lyrics (*The Grapes of Wrath*) to Shakespeare (*Something Wicked This Way Comes*). Make a list of things that remind you of your story, your characters' names, names of places, metaphors and similes you've used, jargon from the character's occupations (teaching, law enforcement, medicine, farming, science), themes, and catchy lines of narration or dialogue from your novel. Just write down everything, even ideas you're sure you won't use. A bad title idea might trigger you to think of one that's perfect.

Although many recent bestsellers have noun or adjective-noun structures ...

- *The Shack*
- *The Host*
- *The Kite Runner*
- *The Bourne Sanction*

... many have more unusual structures ...

- *You've Been Warned*
- *Into the Flame*
- *Play Dirty*

... and some are short, some lengthy ...

- *Barefoot*
- *A Heartbreaking Work of Staggering Genius*

What are your favorite book titles? Some of mine are:

- *Water for Elephants*
- *Carter Beats the Devil*
- *The Subtle Knife*
- *The Grapes of Wrath*

When you discover a great title for your novel, google it. You want to make sure no recent book, movie, play, or TV show used it first. There is no copyright on titles, but you don't want to confuse people. No matter how good and original your choice of titles, remember that the title of your book might still be changed before it comes out. Be open-minded—publishers, editors, and marketing specialists know what will sell.

WHAT TO DO IF YOU CAN'T GET FOCUSED

There's a moment for me, in the daydreaming stage of an idea, that I call the point of no return. When I've created a scene in my head in such detail that it feels real to me, I have to write that novel because I have to write that scene. There's no turning back. If what makes your story worthy still eludes you, and you're not yet convinced that you have to write this book, try one of the following exercises to help you recall, or discover, why your novel deserves to be written.

- **Go back to the beginning.** If you are one of those people who scribbles notes of ideas on little scraps of paper or in a notebook, go back and see what the very first thing was you wrote about this story. What was the original snippet of an idea? It might be a clue to the core of your novel.

- **Look at a favorite.** Choose a favorite author and write down the premise of his best novel. Reviewing what you love about it might remind you of what you love in your own idea.

- **Court your idea.** Write a love letter to your own novel.

- **Chat with your idea.** Dialogue with your novel. Write out the conversation.

- **Ask your idea why it's so special.** Write out an interview with your novel. Ask those tough questions. Be ruthless. Make it cry.

- **Interview other readers.** Find out why your friends and colleagues love the books they love.

- **Poll the professionals.** Research on the Web how successful novelists get started on new books.

- **Fantasize.** What might your fans say about your novel someday in their blogs?

- **Remember your dream.** List at least ten reasons why you want to be a novelist. Then read them back, out loud, in reverse order.

CHAPTER 2

DECIDING HOW TO TELL YOUR STORY

The shortest distance between truth and a human being is a story.
—Anthony de Mello

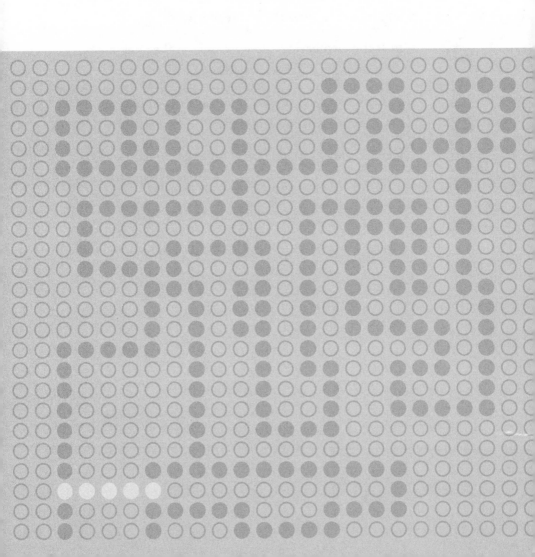

When I was just starting to write my second novel, *The Fetch*, I got excited when I discovered how I would tell the story. While at a restaurant with my sister and two novelist friends, I tried to describe what I meant by "how to tell the story." They said, "The point of view?" I said, "No, it's not point of view." It wasn't *who* would tell the story. I had decided on that long before. "You mean the style?" they asked. And I said, "No. That's not it." I knew it wasn't style. I could use the same prose style I used with my first novel. "Tone?" they asked. But it was more than the attitude or tone of the writing. I explained my idea, how I wanted to tell the story of *The Fetch* like a knight's tale, and they said, "Oh, you mean a device."

Apparently, without realizing what they were called, I had been using storytelling devices for years as shortcuts for getting into my novels. Suddenly I was into devices. *Devices rule!* But before we talk about storytelling devices, we need to talk about point of view (POV), voice, and tone because the four are deeply connected.

POV: WHO SHOULD TELL THE STORY?

Through whose eyes should the readers see your story? It should be the person who has the most to lose, who drives the story, who changes the most, who has the most emotional connection to the outcome of the story. You can have multiple POVs, the same way Barbara Kingsolver told *Prodigal Summer* from several people's viewpoints, but let's look at a single protagonist first. Once you know who your main character is, you can choose to have him narrate the story himself in first person or you can use a third-person narrator. The choices are:

- **First person:** The storyteller is a character who tells the readers only what she feels, sees, knows. *I hated leaving the party early.* This limits what you can show, but it is a very powerful way to tell a story because you become intimate with the main character quickly.

- **Second person:** The narrator uses "you" rather than "I" or "she" and "he" as the pronoun. *You hated leaving the party early.* This is a rare POV to find in a novel. Try it out if you're attracted to it, but I don't recommend it. To me it feels awkward. And it may feel awkward to your readers.

- **Third person:** The narrator uses "he" or "she" pronouns to tell the story. This is probably the most common type, partly because there are so many variations of the third-person narration.

- **Third-person inner limited:** The readers only see and hear what the main character is seeing and hearing. *She hated leaving the party early. She wondered what John was thinking.* Your narration is often flavored by that character's personality almost as if you're hearing her thoughts. I like this choice because I can keep the power and intimacy of focusing on one person's experience, but if my main character doesn't seem like the kind of person who would tell his own story, I don't have to force words out of him in an unnatural first-person POV.

- **Third-person outer limited:** The narrator can watch any character, at any time, but the action being reported is only what can be seen and heard. We never get to know a character's unspoken thoughts. *She paused on the doorstep, then walked away from the house as the party music blared on.* If you're clever you can convey all the necessary emotion of your novel with only actions and dialogue, the way a movie or play shows us only what the characters do and say. But you need to get your characters' feelings out in the open or the story will seem distant and shallow.

- **Third-person omniscient:** This narrator can look into the mind of any character and hear everyone's thoughts. Some omniscient narrators describe only the very basics of what is happening with little judgment, letting the dialogue and action that is being revealed tell the story. *John couldn't understand why Mary was leaving, but he didn't try to stop her. She hated missing the rest of the party, but she had no choice.* Or the omniscient narrator sometimes adds color, perspective, judgment, social commentary, or humor as if the third-person narrator had its own personality. *He could have stopped her, but he was a fool. She could've stayed and danced barefoot with a software salesman, but she was afraid. They were*

intolerably timid creatures that deserved each other.
This gives the writer a lot of freedom, but it can distract from the characters if you're not careful.

- **First-person omniscient:** This narrator, rarely used and mostly in comedies, acts as the writer or storyteller. He speaks to the readers about not only the content of the novel but often about himself and the writing process. *I suppose I could've been kinder and let John and Mary share their first kiss before she ran off to tend to her mother, but I wanted to save that moment for another chapter.* If you have the right story for this kind of thing, it can be charming. But be careful. It's hard to do well. Think of it this way: Ferris Bueller may get away with talking to the audience that is watching his movie, but would you want Rick in *Casablanca* to speak to the camera? Or Dorothy in the movie *The Wizard of Oz*? Most stories are better told from the point of view of the main character (first person) or by a third-person narrator, rather than the supposed author.

As you can see, your POV choice is a major part of your novel. The point of view need not necessarily be the protagonist of the story, though. Sometimes the story needs to be told by an observer to the action. Dr. Watson narrates Sherlock Holmes's cases. In F. Scott Fitzgerald's *The Great Gatsby*, the narrator is Nick Carraway, not Jay Gatsby.

The genre in which you are writing might also influence your choice. Some novels, such as detective mysteries and young adult romances—for example, *The Long Goodbye* by Raymond Chandler and *Twilight* by Stephenie Meyer—work well with a single POV, often in first person. Some comedies with large casts of characters, like Dave Barry's *Big Trouble*, have multiple POVs and use omniscient narration. But some dramas with several important characters have multiple POVs as well, such as Whitney Otto's *How to Make an American Quilt*.

If you read lots of the kind of books you're writing, you already have a pretty good idea of what POVs and narrators work best in that genre, but don't feel trapped. If it's important to you to tell your private eye story from eleven different POVs, and if you have a clear vision of it being brilliant, go for it. You might be on to something.

Recommended Reading

Here are some books with interesting storytelling devices:

- *How to Survive a Robot Uprising* by Daniel H. Wilson: Comic advice based on true science in a do-it-yourself manual format.

- *Dracula* by Bram Stoker: A classic use of multiple character narration through journal entries and letters.

- *The Screwtape Letters* by C.S. Lewis: Readers are given only one half of the correspondence of letters containing fascinating advice about the human race from a veteran devil to his inexperienced nephew.

- *Diary of a Wimpy Kid* by Jeff Kinney: Combines a diary device with a sketchbook device through the cartoons supposedly drawn by the first-person narrator.

- *The Princess Bride* by William Goldman: Allegedly written by S. Morgenstern and creatively edited into the "good parts version" by Goldman. This book provides a unique author interjection device that is irresistible.

DEVELOPING THE NARRATING VOICE

When I was young I used to participate in an annual three-day novel writing event. You had to write an entire first draft of a novel in seventy-two, hours and you went in with only an outline. Whenever I chose a first-person narrator who had a voice like my own, the writing always went faster. The words flowed out of me almost effortlessly, as if I were chatting with a friend. And if you're going to crank out thirty-five pages a day, you really need that flow.

But your story might call for a first-person narrator who does not speak as you do. The novel may be about a turn-of-the-century shoemaker from Liverpool or a Depression era farmer from Alabama. Unless you have friends or relatives with speech patterns acquired from these times and places, you'll have to research the voice. Sounds like a lot of work, but cheer up. Sometimes the best voice is the one that speaks nothing like you. These narrators are colorful and vibrant and get attention from agents and editors.

The same applies to your third-person narrator. If you don't plan to write your novel in first person, you will need to choose your POV. If you've been writing for years, you may have already developed a style that carries through all of your novels. Perhaps you always write with an omniscient POV. If you're new to writing, you may still be developing your style. Perhaps you will experiment with both third-person inner and outer. Your narrator will either speak in a way similar to your natural (personal) voice or very different. It may seem simpler to narrate your novel in your own voice, but watch out. There are dangers on this path.

1. **Your voice may not be strong enough.** The language used and attitude conveyed by your narrator need to be striking, appealing, distinct. If I wrote my novels the way I talk with my friends, I never would've been published. Your narration needs to be more theatrical than your everyday speaking voice. It needs potency and attitude.

2. **You may not hear when you are being inconsistent with your own voice.** We writers change moods and change the way we speak depending

on how we feel—clipped and witty one day, contemplative and poetic the next. But the narration of your book needs to be consistent. This is the attitude that sets the stage for the whole novel. Readers take their cue about what kind of book they are reading from the tone of the narration.

3. **You may cramp your own style.** Unless you're a columnist, it's hard to write in your own voice and not get self-conscious. For this reason, if you want to write a book that talks like you, don't think of it as a story being told by you, but like a story being told by a narrator very much *like* you. So relax. The narrator isn't you. It's a character unto itself. Just play that character.

If you decide to use a narrator who does not speak like you, you'll want to explore that narrator's sound. Ask yourself:

1. **What is appealing about the way your chosen narrator speaks?** Perhaps she is fearless and bold, or quirky and comical. What quality in her voice is the most fun to write?

2. **What is the challenging aspect of this narrator's storytelling?** He may use slang you're not familiar with or have an unusual word order to his cadence because he is speaking in a language other than his native tongue.

3. **Do you need to do research in order to sound like this narrator?** You could rent movies with

characters from this person's homeland or period of history, or check out audio books from the library with narrators who have similar speech patterns.

4. **Can you make up the way this narrator speaks?** If your narrator is from a time so long ago that no one speaks that language anymore (ancient Greece or Rome, for instance), or if she is from the future when slang could have developed in unexpected ways, or if she is from an invented world, then you will be free to create not only the syntax and semantics that sound right to your ear, you can also create your own slang. In *Alphabet of Dreams*, Susan Fletcher created the slang word *savage*, which means approximately the same thing as *great* or *cool*, for a character from the Middle East in the year 1 A.D. It is used in such a natural way, it works perfectly.

Remember, your narrator's voice, along with its tone and attitude, needs to fit your story. The Sherlock Holmes stories would have had the wrong tone if Holmes had narrated them instead of Watson. The stories would probably have been dryer and more analytical. Watson brought a certain kindness with his attitude and perspective that made the complex stories emotionally accessible to the common reader.

You'll save time on rewriting later if you get hooked into your narrator's voice beforehand. This voice needs to sound not only realistic and consistent but interesting to the readers as well. It has to carry you through hundreds of pages.

Here are three additional ways to practice your narrator's voice:

- When you're alone (in the shower, driving to the store, doing the dishes), tell a story in your narrator's voice. It could be a story about anything—what the cat did last night, how you chose your spouse, your favorite high school sports success, your worst bad date.

- When listening to other voices (on TV, on the radio, on the bus), rephrase what you hear as if you were your narrator.

- Take a piece of writing (newspaper article, short story, text book) and read a paragraph aloud. Then either translate it into the voice of your narrator or comment on it in your narrator's voice.

Creating a Distinct Voice

As I've said, the voice in your writing gives your novel its tone and communicates your attitude toward the subject—this mood permeates the whole book. Look at these examples of distinct voices and how they affect the writing.

Informal

There's likely some polished way of starting a story like this, a clever bit of gaming that'd sucker people in surer than the best banco feeler in town. But the truth is that I haven't

got the quick tongue or the slick wit for that
kind of game.

—Stevie, first-person narrator from
Angel of Darkness by Caleb Carr

This voice is period and informal. The narrator is friendly and unpretentious about telling his story. Using this kind of narrator is a good way to get readers comfortable with an unfamiliar place in time quickly and a good way to make the Sherlock Holmesian mystery he will narrate accessible to readers.

This morning before heading to the office I read an in-depth story about Burt and Loni's divorce in *People* magazine. Thus, 1,474,819 brain cells that could have been used toward a formula for world peace were obliterated.

—Dan, first-person narrator from
Microserfs by Douglas Coupland

This voice is informal, but modern. Though this book is a comedy and the Carr book is a mystery, both narrators charm us with their casual spontaneity. Again, an informal narrator makes unfamiliar territory (like a high-tech world) less intimidating.

Emotional vs. Restrained

In the lateness of the night, their two voices reading to each other where she could hear them, never letting a silence divide or

interrupt them, combined into one unceas-
ing voice and wrapped her around as she
listened, as still as if she were asleep. She
was sent to sleep under a velvety cloak of
words, richly patterned and stitched with
gold, straight out of a fairy tale, while they
went reading on into her dreams.

—third-person narrator from *The Opti-
mist's Daughter* by Eudora Welty

This voice is intimate and vulnerable. We hear and feel the
character's unspoken emotions and thoughts in fine detail.
This is a good kind of voice for hooking readers into a story.

As he swung through the air, trembling, he
saw the blackness give way below, like the
parting of clouds, to a deep patch of stars
on the ground. It was the pond, he hoped,
the hole in the woods reflecting the sky. He
judged the instant and let go; he flung himself loose into the stars.

— third-person narrator from
The Living by Annie Dillard

In contrast, this voice is emotionally restrained. The fears
and joys this character experiences are implied, hidden between the lines. This can also be an effective voice, but you
have to be good at it. Dillard's language is beautiful and her
story deftly told, but Dillard is a literary champ. This is a
tricky voice to sustain for three hundred pages. If you go

this way, be careful not to skim over the surface and miss the passion.

Serious vs. Light

How she loved to listen when he thought only the horse could hear. But there was a serpent in her Eden. She searched earnestly in herself to see if she wanted Paul Morel. She felt there would be some disgrace in it. Full of twisted feeling, she was afraid she did want him. She stood self-convicted. Then came an agony of new shame. She shrank within herself in a coil of torture. Did she want Paul Morel, and did he know she wanted him? What a subtle infamy upon her.
—third-person narrator from *Sons and Lovers* by D.H. Lawrence

This voice is intimate and serious. We hear details, uncensored, and we feel the weight of them. An honest voice describing a flawed character from the inside is powerful and appealing.

Then she did a strange, childlike thing: she smelled the key, and licked it. It had a metallic taste that made her shiver slightly, made her feel a surge of Nancy Drew–like excitement.
—third-person narrator from *Divine Secrets of the Ya-Ya Sisterhood* by Rebecca Wells

And here the voice is intimate and light. Again, uncensored, but the details are more lighthearted. In both cases hearing quirky thoughts that the character would probably never admit to out loud works to draw the readers into the story.

Removed vs. Bonded

One hot summer day when he was seven Aaron Firestone sat on his bicycle, staring hypnotically at the traffic on Nassau Street. The street was crowded; the cars seemed hardly to be moving at all. A truck lumbered noisily toward the house. The truck stopped, then started again, but slowly, slowly. Aaron pushed hard on the foot pedal and the bike left the sidewalk and skidded over the curb, down into the hot street. Aaron fell backward, balance gone. The truck braked, stopping, but not before its great wheels rolled up and over Aaron's legs.

—third-person narrator from *Boys and Girls Together* by William Goldman

This voice reports observations in a detached way and lets the readers glean the emotion from it. It's startling how nonchalantly Goldman describes a horrible accident. As readers, our feelings are heightened in a kind of opposition to the voice. This can be profoundly effecting, but it's not easy to pull off. If you think this kind of voice is right for your novel, test it out first to see how it feels.

I threw down the bitten windfall I had been eating, and tilted my head to study the forbidden tree-top boughs where yellow globes hung clustered against the sky. There was one I thought I could reach. The fruit was round and glossy, ripening almost visibly in the hot sun. My mouth watered. I reached for a foothold and began to climb.

—Merlin, first-person narrator from
The Crystal Cave by Mary Stewart

In contrast, this voice is so generous with details that we feel bonded with the narrator; we're in the same skin. We expect to be in accord with this voice throughout the novel.

A Voice That Contrasts With Content

The education bestowed on Flora Poste by her parents had been expensive, athletic and prolonged; and when they died within a few weeks of one another during the annual epidemic of the influenza or Spanish Plague which occurred in her twentieth year, she was discovered to possess every art and grace save that of earning her own living.

—third-person narrator from *Cold Comfort Farm* by Stella Gibbons

With this voice, the humor of the story is enhanced by the seemingly serious language, which is in contrast to the subject matter and to the crazy characters and silly situations that follow. If you long to write like Jane Austen or P.D. Wodehouse, this might be the voice for you.

> My God, what did he want? He certainly wasn't a *pervert*, Tom thought for the second time, though now his tortured brain groped and produced the actual word, as if the word could protect him, because he would rather the man be a pervert than a policeman.
> —third-person narrator from *The Talented Mr. Ripley* by Patricia Highsmith

Here the chilling quality of the story is enhanced by the disarmingly casual language, which is in contrast to the subject matter and deceptions and murders that follow. This is a tricky voice to write well. You have to know your protagonist intimately in order to sustain this kind of flippancy in the face of horror or you'll lose your readers. Note that this is an example of such a close-fitting third-person POV that it feels like first person. Notice the way Highsmith writes what Tom is thinking without always labeling it *thought Tom* in the first sentence of the example. We live inside the protagonist's head for the whole book.

A Voice That Narrates With Two Tones

After an early luncheon, William went to say good-bye to his grandmother. She looked at him with doleful, mad eyes. "Going to London, eh? Well I hardly suppose I shall be alive when

you return. Wrap up warm, dear." It was eter-
nal Winter in Mrs. Boot's sunny bedroom.

All the family who had use of their legs
attended on the steps to see William off. ...
—third-person narrator from *Scoop*
by Evelyn Waugh

Here is a voice that presents humor wrapped in formal language. It is similar to the Austen/Wodehouse/Gibbons voice
except that the humor is dryer, at times bordering on black
comedy. Is it funny or disturbingly dark?

> Some people had sins attached to them like
> second skins, even the sins of their parents.
> Like Anton Immers, the butcher, who was old-
> er than many of their fathers, but everyone in
> town knew that he'd been born three months
> after his parents' wedding. A three-month
> baby. That meant sin. Or like Helga Stamm,
> who was Trudi's age but a bastard because
> her mother hadn't married at all. That skin of
> sin—the town wouldn't let the people take it
> off entirely even though everyone pretended
> it was not there. The town knew.
> —third-person narrator from *Stones*
> *from the River* by Ursula Hegi

Here is a voice that presents poetic insight wrapped in the
informal voice of a child, an effective narration because the
readers seemingly understand more than the narrator.

TONE

Tone is communicated through language but also through what the author chooses to include in the story, what images are emphasized, the setting, and the characters. If your narrator dwells on negative situations, if the setting is depressing, if the characters are nasty or pitiable, the mood will be dark even if the narrator describes these things with lighthearted language. It works the other way as well. If your narrator's voice conveys a tone that is negative it might be counteracted by a pleasant setting and delightful characters. Let's look at some examples of how the wrong tone might throw off your writing.

Here is my own darker-toned take on an excerpt from *Good Omens* by Neil Gaiman and Terry Pratchett:

> Two figures lurked in the ruins that had once been a graveyard. One figure was bent, heavy of trunk and limb. The other thin with a menacing expression. Fog curled between the headstones like the Angel of Death. The two would wait patiently for him all night if they had to.

The actual, lighter version:

> Two of them lurked in the ruined graveyard. Two shadowy figures, one hunched and squat, the other lean and menacing, both of them Olympic-grade lurkers. If Bruce Springsteen had ever recorded "Born to

Lurk," these two would have been on the album cover. They had been lurking in the fog for an hour now, but they had been pacing themselves and could lurk for the rest of the night if necessary, with still enough sullen menace left for a final burst of lurking around dawn.

A heavy tone would have ruined the fun. It is not only the fanciful reference to Bruce Springsteen that adds lightness, but also the comic device of repeating one word into absurdity.

A mock-up of a lighter-toned excerpt from *Sleep, Pale Sister* by Joanne Harris:

> The chill up my back must have been imaginary—my spine isn't exactly functional anymore. The aftermath of my stroke has shrunken to a tiny twitch in my head. I know I am done for—no surprise there. And, honestly, it will be a relief. Still, something in me has gotten used to being alive, if you can call my state living. As the sun starts to rise, I almost imagine I can see in the clouds the face of God frowning at me.

The actual version Harris wrote:

> A sudden panic sends ripples down my ruined spine. I feel the tic that has already frozen half my face begin to twitch again, relentlessly, as if a tiny, furious creature were

imprisoned behind my eye-socket, gnawing its way out. The last card of our game
is Death ... I knew it from the start, but although the looseness in my ribcage is relief,
my brain rebels against annihilation, stupid
tissue screaming out: no no no no! The lid
of night is beginning to lift and beneath it is
the Eye of God with its blank, blue iris and
terrible humour.

A light tone would have robbed this passage of the necessary chill. Here the passage is made disturbing by the use of
extreme imagery (ruined spine, gnawing its way out, screaming) and by unexpected mirroring (the juxtaposition of the
twitch behind the character's eye—a remnant of his severe
stroke—and the daylight sky as the impossibly huge blue of
the eye of God).

If you haven't settled on the tone of your novel, or if the
passages you have already written don't feel right (or if the
writing only feels right in places), try one of the following
exercises.

1. Take a slice of action from your book and try writing it in the opposite tone than you think you
   should use, exaggerated, as wrong as you can get.
   Then try to rewrite it in the exact opposite tone.
   For some reason this double translation often un-
   sticks me and slides me into the right tone.

2. Read aloud a section from a novel that has the
   tone you want to create in your own writing. Do

this right before you start writing or rewriting for the day.

3. Take a novel with the tone you want to emulate and copy out a page by hand, letting the word choices and sentence construction and punctuation and pacing go from that printed page to your eye, into your brain, down your arm, into your pen, and out onto your paper. I don't know why, but it's helped me in the past to take a few minutes and *feel* some great writing go through my body.

THE DEVICE

In the novel *Contact* by Carl Sagan, when Ellie Arroway finally speaks face-to-face with a being from another planet, that being appears in the form of Ellie's father because, it tells her, this makes communicating with her easier and more meaningful. That's also how the device works. The storytelling device is a contrivance, a way to present your novel in an iconic form so the readers will have a deeper experience of the story. A device is part point of view, part style, and part tone, but it's more than that. What makes it a device is all three of those things plus *props*. Device props can be anything from travel tips in *The Accidental Tourist* by Anne Tyler to entomolgy lessons sprinkled throughout Barbara Kingsolver's *Prodigal Summer.*

A device can be invisible, or covert, so subtle that the readers have no idea you are using a device at all. A device can be obvious, or overt, like the journal device in *Bridget Jones's Diary* by Helen Fielding.

The overt device: *Bridget Jones's Diary* could have been told with a traditional first-person POV and been called *The Adventures of Bridget Jones*, but reading her story in short bursts of journaling was the best way to get at the deeply intimate voice and the rather fractured life of that character. The device is tied to the POV—with a diary you have to have the narrator telling her story in writing. It's tied to style—the writing is casual and honest, a private journal. And it's tied to tone—the attitude is both comic and painful because Bridget is a girl of great hope even in the face of disaster. But the device also incorporated overt props. There were not only headings that told us when each entry was being recorded, it also gave us a running list of how many cigarettes, drinks, and pounds were coming and going in Bridget's life.

The covert device: For my novel *A Certain Slant of Light,* I chose a Victorian love story as my device. It was tied to POV—such stories are told from the female lover's point of view. It was tied to style—I adopted an old-fashioned (nineteenth-century) sounding prose style. It was tied to tone—most ghost stories are told like ghost stories, from the point of view of someone being haunted, but this one was from the (first-person) point of view of the ghost herself, and I had her tell her story with the tone of a romance. I had the character Helen focus on the emotions of falling in love and the obstacles on the path to that happy union. But to make my device complete, I gave it the Victorian love story prop of literature. Helen chose her hosts (the chain of people she haunted for over a century) because they were poets and play-wrights and scholars. As soon as she was in a physical body, she took romances from the library. I had people read aloud whenever I could, flowering the manuscript with Shakespeare, Charlotte Brontë, Robert Frost, and Emily Dickinson. But this was a covert device because I doubt if many of my readers could have pointed it out. And that was as I intended. It was something subtle, but the device made all the difference to me as I was writing and I hope added resonance to the book for my readers. When I'm starting a new novel, the writing goes much faster for me once I've latched onto the right storytelling device.

Let's look at a few devices and their props.

1. **The Documentary.** Richard Matheson's novel *Hell House* uses the storytelling prop of labeling each scene with the date and time of day. This gives the impression that it's not only a true story, but that it's an incredibly accurate and scientific one. Recording the actual minutes is effective because the only reason someone would have made note of the exact time is because something disturbing is about to happen.

2. **The Cautionary Tale.** In Charles Dickens's *A Christmas Carol*, the antihero, Ebenezer Scrooge, is not only presented to us as a man gone bad who is saved from his wicked ways by repenting, he is escorted through the stages of his life in an orderly, structured way. By using the props of four Heralds of Danger (Marley's ghost and three other

spirits), Dickens shows Scrooge, and all of us, exactly what went wrong and exactly what Scrooge should have done, step by step, past, present, future. Dickens even named his warning ghosts after their parts of the "How Not To" guide: Past, Present, Yet to Come.

3. **The Knight's Tale.** In my novel *The Fetch*, I used what I call a knight's tale device because the story is told from the point of view of the knight (in this case the Fetch), it is written with a voice, and conveys a tone that call to mind the days of chivalry (emphasizing the romantic pull between passion and duty). I also used several props that are reminiscent of a knight's life: vows, legends, psalms, and the passing of a key, the Fetch equivalent of the sword in a knighting ritual.

4. **The Confession.** The character tells the story as if confessing to something: sins great or small, a hidden identity, etc. In Peter Shaffer's play *Amadeus*, the playwright uses the audience as a prop by having the antihero Salieri speak directly to them as he confesses his sins of artistic jealousy.

5. **The Book of Wisdom.** The story is told as if some great knowledge is being passed along. Susan Fletcher makes use of an effective prop in her novel *Shadow Spinner*. At the beginning of every chapter in this tale of a young woman learning about storytelling from Shahrazad, Fletcher

includes a short passage titled "Lessons in Life and Storytelling."

6. **Scripture.** For *Judas Cross*, a novel-in-progress that won me a modest literary fellowship, I chose a scripture device because the novel was a biblical tale. I decided to use the prop of a fictional Passion play. The medieval theater pieces known as Passion plays were retellings of the books of the New Testament that pertain to the end of Christ's life. I wrote my own mini-Passion play, using similar language and stylized poetry to that of the old plays, and then quoted my own fake play as a prologue, an epilogue, and one line at the opening of every chapter. I made sure I cited the act and scene numbers to add to the authenticity, as if I had based my novel on some lost books of the Bible that had not been known since medieval times.

As I've said, a device is a contrivance. You make it up to suit your purposes. Others before you may have invented or uncovered plot patterns or story structures that have the same name as the device you will create, but a device does not have to conform to any pattern or structure like the examples above. You are inventing your own device, remember? There may already be a hero's journey structure or a plot pattern for a fairy tale, but you don't need to know either of those methods, or the rules they involve, to make up your own fairy tale or hero's journey device. All you need to know is how one of those devices will work for you.

Fun Stuff

- Try this game: Copy down the following devices on slips of paper and put them in a hat. Feel free to make up your own ideas for storytelling devices.

> The Ode
> The Cautionary Tale
> The Knight's Tale
> The Legend
> The Confession
> The Fairy Tale
> Scripture
> The Documentary
> The Book of Wisdom

Draw one at random. Then copy down the following story ideas on slips of paper and make another blind drawing. Again, feel free to make up your own suggestions.

> Golidlocks and the Three Bears
> Little Red Riding Hood
> The Tale of Robin Hood
> *Romeo and Juliet*
> *Hamlet*
> The Life of Abraham Lincoln
> The Life of Elvis Presley
> The Voyage of the *Titanic*

Now put the two elements you drew together and write for five minutes outlining your ideas of how the given story idea could use the given device, including props. But throw them back and start over if you draw "The Voyage of the *Titanic*" with "The Documentary" or "Little Red Riding Hood" with "The Fairy Tale." That would be too close to the normal version. What if you draw "Golidlocks and the Three Bears" and "The Book of Wisdom"? Or "Elvis" and "The Knight's Tale"? Now that's interesting. The point isn't to come up with material for your novel, but to stir your creativity as a conjurer of stories, and to develop mastery over original and intriguing storytelling devices.

- Go somewhere out in the world where there is a lot happening—a popular dog park, a shopping mall, a high school football game, a Saturday farmers market—and use your digital camera without looking. Take ten or twenty shots without bothering to check where you are aiming. When you get home, look through the images. Choose the most intriguing and write a story premise based on that picture.

Now that you know what a device is, and that you're free to play with them all you like, let's practice by making up some devices and applying them to the tale of "The Tortoise and the Hare." You know the story. The hare is a much faster runner, but he's cocky. He's so sure he'll win the race that he takes a nap in the middle of it. The tortoise is not swift, but he never stops. He just keeps walking, and slow and steady wins the race.

Now, let's create some storytelling devices and try them out. These are just examples—be creative.

- **The Ode.** This is a tale of praise or adoration for a person, place, or thing. The praise can come from a secret admirer, a best friend, a lowly fan, or an equal. The ode can be expressed as if everyone already loves this story, or as if the value of this treasure were never known until now. Props could range from lines of actual odes (or made-up ones) to chapter openers comparing this tortoise or race to others that pale in comparison.

  Let's have the tale told by Tortoise's wife, looking back on the race, speaking of Tortoise affectionately. We'll start every chapter with a couplet from the invented "Ballad of Slow Foot," a love poem written by Mrs. Tortoise, the narrator. "Oh Mossy Back, beloved mate, of sturdy leg and courage great ..."

- **The Legend or Myth.** The epic story of Tortoise, the larger-than-life hero, destined to defeat the infamous Hare of Darkness, may be told by a scholar who has researched this amazing creature all his life. The language might be academic. A tone of awe could infuse this telling. Props are references to items that still remain as proof of this miraculous event: the Heroes Rock where the race began, the Tree of Foolishness under which the Hare took his respite, and the Field of Triumph where the race ended. There may even be a term, a made-up euphemism, that derives from this legend. *That is why even today the underdog in a race is sometimes called the sly shell.*

- **The Fairy Tale.** This is like the legend device but more fanciful, magical even. The storyteller can be more Mother Goose-ish. The language might be simple but the tone mysterious. A sense of the magical is sustained with props like spells or incantations. Or fairy prophecies come true. The storyteller could be quite old, from the days when there truly were fairies hiding in every flower. *Shall I tell you, my great- and very great-grandchildren, of the prince who was enchanted by the Queen of the Brownies, who was turned into a crawling beast and forced to carry his house upon his back?*

The well of storytelling devices is bottomless because your imagination is limitless. How about the book report? The operations manual? The rock ballad? The tabloid? The cookbook? The fan club? You take it from here.

But, you may ask, what happens if I choose the wrong device? You'll feel it. Trying to employ the device will be a struggle, the writing will slow down, the characters will seem out of place, the tone will seem awkward, the props will stick out like a hand of sore thumbs. And that's exactly the opposite of the way it feels when you latch onto the perfect device. The writing will flow, the characters will bloom, the props will delight you.

Here is my best advice to you on how to use your story-telling device after you decide on it:

1. **Make sure your POV matches your device.** Bridget Jones was the perfect person to write a journal because she was trying to create and stick to some New Year's resolutions. Ask yourself how your device and POV help each other.

2. **Make sure your writing style matches your device.** If your chosen device is legend but your prose sounds like Mickey Spillane, there may be a problem. Try another device or try going without one.

3. **Make sure your tone matches your device.** Is your tone formal, but the device informal? Light tone but dark device? As you write your first chapter using your device, does it feel awkward or perfect? If it doesn't feel right, start over. What drew you to that device in the first place?

4. **Open with the device.** To establish the device, even if it is subtle and covert, make sure you start with a strong demonstration from the first page. Set the language and tone right up front. Think of the "Lesson" at the opening of *Shadow Spinner* or the first entry in *Bridget Jones's Diary*.

5. **If you start a pattern, keep it up.** This will help sustain the effect. If your prop is to label your scenes with the date and time of day, like in *Hell House*, do it consistently for every new scene. Don't let your props fade away.

6. **Make sure you end with the device.** The openings and endings of all novels should have something in common. If you use a device, look at how you started page one and try to write your last page as the second bookend in the set.

7. **Avoid a cliché with the right choice of device.** If you write a Cinderella kind of story with a fairy tale device or the story of King Arthur with a legend device, it might be too obvious and come off as cliché. Not only can you avoid being corny and cliché by using the perfect device, you can hit on a fresh, original combination. Imagine how much more interesting a Cinderella tale might be told if through a gossip column device. What unexpected device might you use to tell the legend of Arthur?

But, just because using devices has helped me with speed and quality in my writing, there's no rule that says you have to use a device at all. If none of the above sounds like you or your story, and if no idea for a new device comes to you, don't worry. Write your story the best way you can. Trust yourself. Write it the way you love to hear it.

CHAPTER 3

CROSSHAIRS MOMENTS

*Your pivotal moment of change is the key moment
you are building to.*

—Dona Cooper

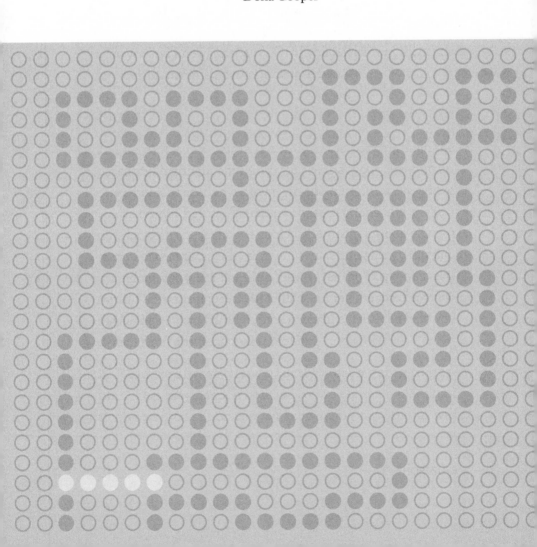

The crosshairs of a story, like the crosshairs in the scope on a rifle, must be precisely aimed at your target—that most pivotal moment in your plot. The *crosshairs* moment, to be exact. And it's crucial to note, especially before we get too far along, that there are different levels of crosshairs moments: the *story* crosshairs moment and the *chapter* crosshairs moments.

Your overarching story crosshairs moment falls on the biggest turning point in your story, often the action's climax. Your individual chapter crosshairs moments, on the other hand, are the most important things that happen in each chapter. They fall on turning points as well, crucial junctures where the plot or character arc (sometimes both) changes direction or makes a leap in energy. The reason you need to make sure you know exactly where your crosshairs lie is because these are the points you'll write toward and away from. These critical moments are what you need to showcase, the moments that create the shape of your story.

IDENTIFYING THE STORY CROSSHAIRS MOMENT

Naming crosshairs in a book you are reading can be subjective. For instance, in *The Dead Zone* by Stephen King, *you* may feel that the overarching crosshairs moment is when the protagonist, Johnny Smith, first discovers the "dead zone," which demonstrates that his premonitions may not necessarily *have* to happen. This, you may believe, is the story crosshairs moment because it gives a new significance to Johnny's gift of prophecy. It's a discovery that will lead to the climax and conclusion of the book. But your friend might choose the moment Johnny poses the philosophical question: "If you had a time machine, would you go into the past and kill Hitler?" (Only for Johnny it's not so theoretical.) Maybe your friend argues that this is the real story crosshairs moment because it's when the protagonist explains the potential power of the "dead zone" to the readers—if Johnny can assassinate a politician that he can see will one day destroy the world, his gift will have a profound benefit for humankind. *Subjectivity.*

When it comes to your *own* writing, though, you need to be able to identify the main story crosshairs moment with precision because (1) it's your story, (2) you need to build up tension to that dramatic moment, and (3) you need to let that tension ripple outward in widening circles of impact. Let your readers get wrapped up in the story and carried away. Let them debate your storytelling crosshairs, the way you and your friends may have fought over the *Dead Zone* moment. But you need to know where that moment is.

Let's look at how Stephen King wrote toward and away from the crosshairs in *The Dead Zone.*

Building to the Story Crosshairs Moment

To make sure that your readers feel the intended impact of the crosshairs moment of your novel, you need to make sure you have prepared them. The readers need to have made the hard journey to this moment alongside your protagonist so that it feels as powerful to them as it does to the character. They need to understand how everything involved with this moment works so that, when the moment arrives, they are thinking, "Ah ha! Of course," rather than "Say what now?" And they need to know exactly what hangs in the balance as this moment unfolds.

1. **Make sure the readers understand the importance of the moment.** In *The Dead Zone*, King takes the readers through several grueling adventures where Johnny deals with his unwanted gift of prophecy and feels unsatisfied, even tortured, by his abilities. This makes finding a grand purpose for his gift meaningful. This is the reason we have come with him through all his trials.

2. **Make sure the readers understand how the rules work so the moment needs no explanation.** When we get to the crosshairs moment, we not only know the way Johnny's visions come to him (we've seen many examples), we also know these episodes are taking their toll on him physically. He can't go on forever making prophecies—it's killing him.

3. **Make sure all necessary backstory is in place so the readers feel what's at stake.** In *The Dead Zone*, the readers are well educated about the man Greg Stillson. We know he's evil. We know he's fooled millions of people. We feel the full impact of the possibility of Johnny risking everything to stop this man.

Now, as you plan your own crosshairs moment, look for ways to prepare your readers. Show them the struggle your hero goes through to climb to this moment. Set up the rules of your reality—make the moment seem inevitable, if you can. Lay out the exposition gradually and early on to sustain the tension over the outcome of this moment.

Echoing the Story Crosshairs Moment

Much like building to the crosshairs, you also need to make sure everything that happens after the crosshairs moment is affected by the event. Everything in the book should be tied to this moment. It can't be a temporary thing. And the aftermath needs to feel right for the kind of story you're telling.

1. **Tie the crosshairs moment to all the subplots and plot points that follow, including character arcs.** Johnny is risking his life, his reputation (he will be seen as a crazy assassin afterward), and his relationship with the woman he loves. If your crosshairs scene is the most important moment in the book, the readers need to see the impact running through the rest of the pages that follow.

2. **The emotional shift that happened in your crosshairs moment has to remain true for your character.** If your hero gathers enough personal strength at that important crosshairs moment to decide to make a sacrifice, like Johnny did, then for the rest of the book the readers need to see that strength in him. Johnny owns his resolve for the

rest of the novel. We can see and feel that he is a changed man.

3. **The tone of the novel should match the crosshairs.** If your lighthearted adventure has a sobering crosshairs moment, make sure you don't jump back into a playful tone as if nothing happened. If your gritty mystery has a heartwarming crosshairs moment, don't go on as if that important warming were a mirage. After the crosshairs moment in *The Dead Zone,* there is an appealing energy that continually calls back to mind that new resolve: *Maybe I can save the world.*

As you write your overarching crosshairs moment and the scenes that follow, make sure every page echoes that moment. Look at how each character is affected. Demonstrate how everything has changed. And make sure the tone of your crosshairs moment, and the effect it has on your subplots and characters, fits the overall tone of the book.

Writing Your Own Overarching Crosshairs Moment

Now that we've looked at how to write toward and away from your story's crosshairs moment, let's look at the moment itself. First you'll need to identify the overarching crosshairs moment because, as I've mentioned, if you get this wrong it will throw off the whole plot. With that in mind, here are four tips to help you clarify the crosshairs of your novel.

1. **Write down your theme.** Something about this theme should have a strong link to your crosshairs. If "war is hell" is your theme, your crosshairs moment might be when your protagonist soldier puts down his gun and goes on strike at the risk of a court-martial.

2. **Write down the central problem in your novel.** Something about this problem should point the way to your crosshairs moment. If your story problem is that a woman needs to get her sister out of a dangerous country, then the crosshairs moment may be when the protagonist makes a hard choice about what she'll give up to get her sister a safe passage out.

3. **Write down the most driving force inside your hero.** Something about this desire, fear, or wound will point you to your crosshairs moment. If your antihero is greedy, the crosshairs moment may come when his greed almost destroys him and he either implodes or has an epiphany.

4. **Write down your central setting.** This may or may not imply a crosshairs moment, but be open-minded. If it's a classroom, something will be learned. If it's a courtroom, justice or injustice will be served. If it's the bedroom of a married couple, there will be a reunion or a parting. See if your setting doesn't show you the way.

Now that we know how to identify the crosshairs, let's talk about how to actually write it. A great crosshairs moment starts with a powerful need in your main character that is so strong the readers feel it. What does your protagonist want desperately? What is his goal? There have to be significant blocks to this goal. Whoever or whatever is working against your character needs to make it seem almost impossible for that goal to be met. Make sure in each step of the scene, in each paragraph, you show the readers what is happening, how this feels (internally) to the protagonist, his outward reaction to what has happened, and the new reaction this creates. And unless this is the climax to the whole novel, and that novel has a happy ending, the goal should remain unresolved.

The protagonist will come off as dynamic because he is fighting to achieve the goal, and the readers will keep turning pages because of the tension that this unresolved passion creates. But be careful with the protagonist's internal and external reactions. You want to give the readers time to feel the emotion the character is experiencing, but you don't want to slow down the pace. And remember, you are not just giving your readers an emotional experience; you're giving them the most important emotional experience in the whole story. This is what it's all about. If an actress were reading the script based on your novel, this is the scene that would make her want to play the part of your hero. If you're writing horror, here is where your hero faces that horror. If you're writing romance, this is where the love opens or breaks the heart. Whatever your readers have come to you for, here's where you give them what you promised you would deliver.

Creating the Pinpoint of the Story Crosshairs Moment

A story's crosshairs moment, as we've discussed, is the most important thing that happens in the whole novel. The *pinpoint* of that moment is the most significant sentence or phrase in the telling of the crosshairs moment; it's the crux of that moment. Let's say your novel has a crosshairs moment that happens in an argument during which a man decides to leave his wife. The crosshairs is the moment the man realizes his marriage is over, it's hopeless, but the pinpoint is the moment—a kind of mini-moment—when his wife laughs after admitting she'd betrayed him. That's what really does it for him, the sound of her laughter. For the character it was a very specific detail, and for you as the writer it becomes a carefully worded sentence. There may even be one key word that is the pinpoint word. Let's look at overarching crosshairs examples from well-known stories and find the pinpoints.

When we look at the following examples, remember, naming crosshairs in literature is subjective. Don't bite my head off if you disagree and would have chosen a different moment.

Jane Eyre by Charlotte Brontë

The overarching crosshairs is the moment when Mr. Rochester, having become the man he needs to be in order to love Jane as an equal, finally proposes. The pinpoint of the exchange is when Jane, who still doubts his sincerity, reads his soul. *Mr. Rochester, let me look at your face.* It is a moment symbolic of Jane's whole journey. She was never seeking safety or wealth or praise or amusement. She was always seeking a companion of the soul, her true equal.

Hamlet by William Shakespeare

The overarching crosshairs of the story come in Act III, scene iii, when Hamlet wants to avenge his father by killing his uncle, but hesitates. The fact that he can't do it is what makes the story and character so interesting. The pinpoint moment, the key to that hesitation, is that if Hamlet were to kill his uncle while the man is praying for forgiveness, the uncle would go to heaven. This does not seem fair. The idea of heaven is also the key to all of Hamlet's questions about life: If my father was killed without having prepared his soul through prayer, is he barred from heaven? What is man if not a heavenly being? If I took my life, in which kind of place would I find myself?

Les Misérables by Victor Hugo

In the overarching crosshairs from this epic tale, our hero, Jean Valjean, who is living under an assumed name, gives up his new life of respect and freedom when he takes responsibility for his past sins in order to save a life. The pinpoint of this moment is his declaration in court: *Release the accused. Your honor, order my arrest. He is not the man whom you seek; it is I. I am Jean Valjean.* This is not only a shock to the other characters and the readers—not to mention a noble thing for our hero to do—but it also symbolizes the novel's most important message about being a worthy human being.

The Miracle Worker by William Gibson

In the overarching crosshairs from this play, Helen Keller has a breakthrough when she makes the connection between objects and the words for them. To give you a little background, Helen spills the water from a pitcher during one of her tantrums. Her tutor, Annie Sullivan, takes her outside to refill it at the water pump in the yard. Annie spells the word *water* into Helen's hand, while the water runs over their fingers. Helen has been resistant to learning words, but now remembers having spoken the word "water" as a baby; she makes the connection and begins to touch things, urging Annie to spell her the words for them. Helen repeats the words in finger spelling into palm—*ground, water pump, porch step*. Helen's parents join her and they celebrate with tears and embraces.

Helen gropes, feels nothing, turns all around, pulls free, and comes, with both hands groping, to find Annie. She encounters Annie's thighs; Annie kneels to her, Helen's hand pats Annie's cheek impatiently, points a finger, and waits, and Annie spells into it. And here is the pinpoint of that crosshairs moment. Annie says the word "teacher." Helen spells it back to Annie, who nods and says again, "teacher." More important even than the first word Helen learns or speaks, this word, symbolizing her relationship with the person who brought her that language, is the pinpoint of the overarching crosshairs moment.

When I write the pinpoint moments in the crosshairs of my books, it reminds me of the way an actor relishes the best lines he is given in a play or movie and tries out several ways of playing the most important line. He chooses the best version. I love choosing the best version of my pinpoint lines.

Recommended Reading

- *The Writer's Guide to Writing Your Screenplay* by Cynthia Whitcomb: Chapter twenty-one, "Climaxes," to learn about creating the climax in a story.

- *Writing the Breakout Novel* by Donald Maass: Chapters six, seven, and nine for great advice on plotting.

IDENTIFYING CHAPTER CROSSHAIRS MOMENTS

Every chapter needs to have its own center of power, and that's where chapter crosshairs moments come into play.

Chapter crosshairs are like miniature versions of the over-arching crosshairs; they fall at key turning points in the plot. As the most important moment in a given chapter, this mini-crosshairs moment is what you want to write toward and away from within the scope of each individual chapter (unless that moment is the last moment in the chapter; in that case you'll just build to it).

When you look at the outline of the book you are about to write, or at the draft you are rewriting, think about what makes the chapter necessary and meaningful. Begin to mark the crosshairs of each chapter, until you end up with something like the following fictional example. One phrase, or even one word, might be enough for you to label each chapter's crosshairs.

- **Crosshairs of the whole story:** Jill leaves her father to start a new life.

- **Chapter one:** Jill discovers that her mother didn't leave her father for another man as her father had claimed for years; instead he had driven her away.

- **Chapter two:** Jill's father has an apparent attack, a fit that cannot be linked to a heart attack or stroke, but it frightens her.

- **Chapter three:** Her father fires the nurse without apparent cause.

- **Chapter four:** Jill gives up her job in order to stay at home and care for her father.

- **Chapter five:** Jill meets a guy she is attracted to.

- **Chapter six:** Jill finds that her father sent away the new nurse.

- **Chapter seven:** Jill, trapped caring for her father, turns down a date with the man she is interested in.

- **Chapter eight:** When Jill confronts her father, he has another "attack."

- **Chapter nine:** After learning the truth, Jill leaves her father.

- **Chapter ten:** Jill comes back after a year to find her father little changed.

By now you might be thinking, so what? How does knowing the most important moment in each chapter help me? It helps because when you know that in chapter seven everything should revolve around the turning down of the date, let's say, rather than the father trying to bribe Jill with a present or getting a clear medical report from the lab, you'll know better how to shape and flavor your writing to emphasize that most vital moment. The crosshairs mold the book; the mini-crosshairs, or chapter crosshairs, mold each chapter. The themes, story problems, character arcs, metaphors and similes, pacing—everything that goes into telling the story—develops from these moments.

The Influence of Turning Points

As I've mentioned, crosshairs fall on turning points in the story. There are many kinds of turning points that serve different functions. The biggest, most dynamic turning points tend to come at the beginning of act two (of a typical three-act structure), at the beginning of act three, and at the climax, but there should be at least one minor turning point in every chapter. We assume that the minor turning point in the first act (like Luke Skywalker's aunt and uncle being killed in *Star Wars*) will carry less importance in the long run than the big turning point at the climax of the story in act three (Luke destroying the Death Star), and that's as it should be. It's what makes stories interesting: a rollercoaster ride of big and little moments building to the finish.

There are a variety of different types of turning points or chapter crosshairs moments. For instance:

• **New information is introduced.** In *The Scarlet Pimpernel* by Baroness Emmuska Orczy, during a grand ball at the stroke of midnight, the readers discover the identity of the Pimpernel (a revelation to the readers but still a mystery to the villain). These kinds of moments energize the story. They add tension to the story because they usually throw new obstacles into the characters' paths.

• **A character has a change of heart or mind.** For instance, in Charles Dickens's *A Christmas Carol*, Scrooge takes a small step toward enlightenment when he asks the Ghost of Christmas Present whether Tiny Tim will live. (Tim is a child Scrooge knew nothing of and cared nothing for at the beginning of the story.) Changes of heart or mind either create tension, as in a good guy turning to the dark side and becoming an enemy, or they release tension, as when a stubborn or evil character finally does the right thing.

• **An action creates a dramatic reaction.** In Margaret Mitchell's *Gone With The Wind*, when Scarlett is assaulted after she insisted on doing business alone in a dangerous part of the country, it sets in motion a retaliation that injures Ashley and takes the life of Frank Kennedy. These kinds of turning points increase the tension in the story because they tend to either accentuate the conflict between the protagonist's goal and the opposing forces or illustrate a flaw in an antihero that foreshadows disaster.

• **A misunderstanding takes place.** In Shakespeare's *Romeo and Juliet*, Romeo misses receiving the message that Juliet will be waiting for him in her family's tomb, drugged and asleep. This misunderstanding leads to a double suicide. These moments add great tension and are good for keeping readers up all night in order to find out how this mistake will be resolved.

• **A character's emotions deflate rather than break.** In *One Flew Over the Cuckoo's Nest* by Ken Kesey, the joy of an unauthorized party is flattened for the mental patients when their nurse interrupts and confronts one of the most fragile inmates with the dreaded idea: "What would your mother say?" This kind of jolt can be effective for increasing the tension.

• **A character's emotions break.** In Dickens's *Nicholas Nickleby*, Nicholas is pushed over the edge and is driven to stop the beating of a crippled boy by turning the whipping stick on the evil schoolmaster. Because we have wanted this to happen for pages and pages, it is very satisfying. But an emotional break can also cause tension when a character we like and are afraid will crumble breaks down at a dangerous junction in the plot, leaving him vulnerable.

• **Power shifts from one character or group to another.** This was the case in the film *The Great Escape*; the prisoners at a POW camp are outwardly celebrating the success of their still (which makes booze from potatoes) and inwardly celebrating their imminent escape through a series of tunnels they are digging. The festivities are interrupted when their Nazi captors discover one of the tunnels. At this turning point one prisoner makes a desperate break for the fence and is shot down. Without moving an inch, the prisoners who are standing in the center of the yard go from toasting each other as if they were victorious heroes to being trapped and defeated. Like the character changing his mind or heart, this kind of shift either creates tension or releases tension depending on if the power shift puts the protagonist on top or at the bottom.

In the novel *Mystic River* by Dennis Lehane, police officers Whitey Powers and Sean Devine suspect Dave Boyle in the murder of a young woman. Whitey has Dave's car towed so they can search it, pretending it was stolen. Whitey is sure he has cornered Dave when blood is found in the car, but during the interrogation the tables turn, creating the crosshairs of the chapter. Dave points out that apparently he couldn't have been the killer.

> "You filled out the report, Sergeant."
> "What report?" Whitey said.
> Sean saw it coming and thought, Oh shit,
> he's got us.

"The stolen car report," said Dave.

"So?"

"So," Dave said, "the car wasn't in my possession last night. I don't know what the car thieves used it for, but maybe you want to find out, because it sounds like they were up to no good."

Your turning point may not look like other authors' turning points. One writer might place the crosshairs moment during the phone call where the hero first hears that his grandmother has died. Another writer might make the protagonist an obsessive-compulsive who will wear only red, and that author might place the crosshairs at the moment the character takes off his red T-shirt and puts on a black dress shirt for the funeral. The crosshairs/turning point moments should grow organically from your plot and characters.

Filtering Keepers From Tossers

If you can't find the crosshairs in a chapter, look again. You might have hidden the most important part of that passage beneath a slush of insignificant action. And are you sure the chapter actually belongs in the book? Should it be shortened and combined with the following chapter? Is it truly necessary? Perhaps it does belong, but it's missing a significant element. Maybe some paragraphs are chaff. As my sister tells her screenwriting students, if you can take something out of the script and the story still works, it has to go. If you can tell which scenes should be cut from looking at your outline, great, but if not, don't worry. You'll begin to find the passages that need cutting organically as you write.

It could be a chapter doesn't seem to have crosshairs, but it still contains some information that needs to be conveyed somehow. The information might fit into a more dynamic chapter. Or that passage might be better if summarized. Try summarizing it and see. We'll look more closely at how to write summary in chapter five.

When I was an English major and wanted to make sure my papers were well structured and tightly written, I would go through the first draft and write in the margin a word or phrase that was a tiny summary of each paragraph. If I had trouble choosing a word or phrase that was an accurate description, I knew that paragraph was either unnecessary or needed focus. When I was rewriting *A Certain Slant of Light*, I tried the same thing with my fiction. In this way I could see where there was an unnecessary paragraph and cut it, or shorten it and combine it with another paragraph. It also helped me see where the most important paragraph was in each chapter. If you've already got a first draft down, try this exercise. Write one word next to every paragraph reminding you why that passage is in the book. It will probably become clear at once where the chapter's crosshairs lie. Everything in that chapter needs to lead to that moment and away from it.

TURNING ALL CROSSHAIRS MOMENTS INTO GREAT MOMENTS

Crosshairs moments, both the overarching crosshairs and the chapter crosshairs, can become great moments—those gems your fans talk about passionately. "Oh, my God, I couldn't believe it when …" or "Didn't you love the part where …" You get the idea. Some great moments make us cry, either from sorrow or joy. Some are frightening; they shock us or make the readers' skin crawl with tension. Some arouse desire. Some make us smile or even make us fall off the couch in laughter. (I admire comic writers. I'm not one.) And some great moments simply make books worth reading. An injustice is righted, a race is won, a search is complete, a villain is sent packing, a character stands up for himself, an innocent is set free … and we celebrate with the characters.

Perhaps you have discovered the crosshairs in one of your chapters, but the passage doesn't feel powerful enough yet. How can you make that crosshairs moment into a great moment? Here are three enhancing techniques:

• **Raise the stakes.** If your crosshairs moment is about a character losing a job, raise it up to losing a career. If your hero might fall from a window and break his leg, maybe it should be a seventh-floor window that would mean a broken neck. After trying everything from theft to blackmail, Edward Zanni is finally accepted to Juilliard at the end of Marc Acito's *How I Paid for College*, one of those moments that make books worth reading. Edward won't simply have to go to community college if he fails to get into Juilliard; his life dreams will be smashed. The stakes are huge because he is so bonded with his goal. To fail would mean to cease being Edward.

Another moment that makes books worth reading is from *To Kill a Mockingbird* by Harper Lee. The villain, Bob Ewell, spits in the face of our hero, Atticus Finch. If Atticus were to retaliate, it would feel as if there were no hope for the world. Because of the extreme racial unrest in the community and the pressure laid upon Atticus as a lawyer defending a black man who is on trial for allegedly raping Ewell's daughter, his actions carry great weight. When Atticus restrains himself and does not strike back at the man, when he is strong enough to turn the other cheek, it feels to the readers as if humanity has been redeemed. The stakes are the highest because they are on the spiritual level.

• **Set up your readers.** If you want your crosshairs moment to feel more intense, make sure the audience has been thinking about it for pages and pages. If you want them to shiver at your ghost appearing across the swimming pool, have someone (the pool boy, the pet dog) already have sensed something wrong at the deep end. If you want the readers to cheer when your characters kiss, have the would-be lovers want to kiss, almost kiss, long beforehand. In Stephen King's *Bag of Bones*, while in a dream, Mike Noonan seems to have sex simultaneously (or perhaps interchangeably) with his dead wife, a young woman he hardly knows, and the ghost of a blues singer, a great moment of the erotic kind. Because King carefully sets up the facts that Mike misses his wife painfully, finds himself attracted to a much younger woman he has only just met, suspects his house is haunted, and is experiencing such devastating writer's block that it makes him ill, the dream scene crackles with sexual intensity.

When the long-suffering Ignatius Reilly and his mother have a little car accident, a great comic moment in John

Kennedy Toole's *A Confederacy of Dunces*, it's especially funny because Toole makes sure the police officer who comes to the scene of the accident is the same one who had dealt with Ignatius in the unfortunate hot dog–eating incident.

• **Exaggerate the contrast.** If in your comedy a bull runs through a feed store, make it a china shop. If your villain is creepy because he wears a cheerful T-shirt with flowers on it while he blows up a building, make it a happy face shirt. Don't use grays; go dark black and bright white. Circus performer Walter grieves, certain he has lost his beloved dog, a tearjerker of a moment in Sara Gruen's *Water For Elephants*. The scene is especially effective because of the contrast between Walter's gruff attitude and foul language and the idea of him sobbing over his lost pup. It makes him suddenly childlike: *"She's all I got."*

In a great moment of the chilling variety, serial killer Gretchen bonds with her captive victim, Archie, in Chelsea Cain's *Heartsick*. The contrast between her lovely face, her sweet voice, her calm attitude, and her actions (forcing Archie to drink drain cleaner) make the scene particularly memorable.

○ ● ○

The more glory or defeat the readers anticipate, the longer the readers have been thinking about what might happen. The more striking the contrasts in the scene, the more powerful your great moments will be.

Fun Stuff

- Go through your movie collection (you can also get several from the public library and a few from rental stores) and choose your favorite moments in your favorite movies. Invite some friends over for a "clips party." Have your guests choose a favorite movie moment to bring with them.

- Imagine your novel as a movie. What moments would be in the preview? If it were up for an Oscar, what crucial moment would they screen for the audience?

- Read out loud your favorite crosshairs from plays, novels, essay collections, or books of poetry. You may be surprised how stimulated and ready to write your own great moments you'll feel after this kind of warm-up.

CHAPTER 4

SHORTCUT TO THE SCENE

*It's really important for writers to remember to reawaken
the reader to the experience of the senses, to put the reader
physically in the character and in the story.*

—Janet Fitch

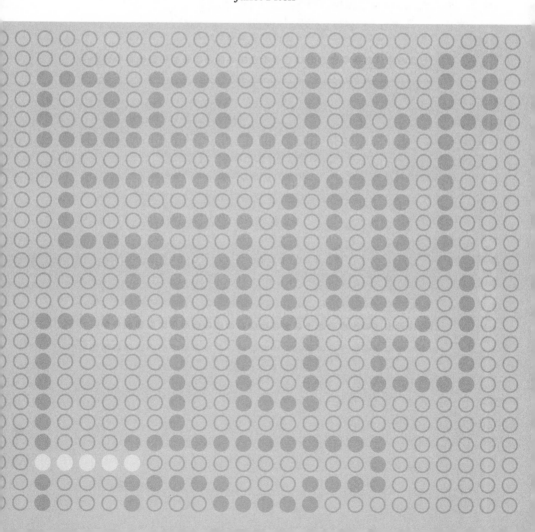

I'm a list maker. I write lists of things to do today, things to put off until tomorrow, grocery lists, things to buy when my ship comes in, and things to put in my novels. Which is probably why I came up with this exercise, the "Shortcut to the Scene." One day I made a list of things that needed to happen in the next scene I was planning to write in my current novel. This list included basic actions (things along the lines of John meets Mary for coffee, finds out they had the same anonymous phone message) and general internal changes (such as Mary stays aloof to John's advances; John feels drawn to Mary despite her coolness).

Then I made a list of what I anticipated the characters would say in the scene, the dialogue. I was working from an outline for the novel, but the scene I was about to write was not outlined in much detail. I listed the dialogue, without bothering to write in the quotation marks or the "he said"/"she said" stuff. This was just a list, after all, just something to remind me of what needed to be said in the scene. I think I separated the dialogue from the narrative stuff because the description in the scene would be written in the narrator's voice and the dialogue would be in the characters' voices. (I was using a third-person POV.) For whatever reason, in my own brain it helped me think about the makeup of the scene in a clearer way.

And so now I had two nice, neat little lists. These were organized, thinker lists. Left-brain lists. To-do lists of what needed to happen in the scene and things that needed to be said. And that was fine.

But I was such a list lover that I also wanted to make a list of the right-brain things that would go into my scene.

If the first two lists included general things like plot points, character development, setups, payoffs, and conflict, I wanted to make a third list that included the subtleties in the prose such as metaphors, similes, descriptions of the senses, and the details that would reflect the characters' emotions and the story's themes. I wanted to list the creative, illogical parts of the scene. But as I tried to list them slowly and thoughtfully, in the manner I had created the two logical lists, I found I couldn't do it. I was trying to make a right-brain list in a left-brain style. So I started over.

This time I just started writing as fast as I could, brainstorming about the emotions, senses, details, the beauty of the scene I was about to write. I didn't worry about punctuation or spelling or typos. I didn't worry about writing full sentences or about organizing my thoughts. I just spewed out whatever came into my head. After about ten minutes of writing I had a long paragraph, almost a full page, of right-brain thoughts. Not all of the ideas were useful, but many parts were very helpful. A few bits were great.

Now I had listed both the logical stuff and the illogical stuff that scenes are made of. I had typed the three parts in one document, with no page breaks, and it all fit on one page. To make the three parts more visually distinct, I changed the type on the second and third parts. I left the "what needs to happen" list in regular type, put the "dialogue" list in bold, and the "free-writing" section—like a brainstorm but I call it a heartstorm because it's more about feeling than thinking—I put in italics.

I printed this page out and was pleased with how I had captured all three concepts on one piece of paper. I put it next to my computer and started to write the scene with this exercise as a guide. And it worked great. I was writing the scene fast and it was coming out good. Really good, in fact.

This "Shortcut to the Scene" exercise is about planning out your scene in advance so you can write it quickly and with third- (or fifth-) draft brilliance the first time around. The exercise provides you with a kind of cheat sheet for writing each scene. But before I take you through writing your own "Shortcut to the Scene," let's talk a little bit about writing scenes.

In some ways, a scene is unlimited. It can be a dozen pages long or less than a page. It can involve a single character or many. There can be one per chapter or several. The scene can be mostly dialogue or contain none. Most scenes take place in a single setting, but some contain multiple settings (for example, where a conversation is taking place while characters travel from one setting to another). But four things that make a scene a scene:

1. **Characters do and say things in real time.** If it weren't real time, if the actions were explained outside of real time, it would be a summary.

2. **There is a beginning, a middle, and an end.** Each scene is like a miniature story. A good scene sets up a goal, builds to a conflict, and leaves something unfinished. You don't want to tie off loose ends at the close of a scene because you want the readers to feel compelled to read the next scene.

3. **A scene must have a purpose.** The scene is developing or introducing one or more characters, providing new information, developing the theme, creating a mood, or creating or sustaining dramatic tension. A good scene is multipurpose and does several of these things.

4. **A scene needs to move the story along.** Think of a good story as a staircase, the top of the stairs being the climax and conclusion of the novel. Each scene is a step. You need to add something to the story (a revelation, a new obstacle, a turning point, a new clue in the mystery) with each scene. That's why multipurpose scenes work so well—they move the story along faster.

STEP I: THE SCENE OUTLINE

To try the "Shortcut to the Scene" exercise, first you must write down what needs to happen in the scene: the goal, the conflict, what will remain unresolved. This includes information that needs to be communicated. You don't need to go into a lot of detail unless it's vital to the plot. Put down the essentials, but leave yourself space to be creative. One paragraph is usually fine, even if the scene will be several pages long.

Here's an example from a scene shortcut I wrote for *The Fetch*. The protagonist, Calder, has thirteen-year-old Alexis and his seventeen-year-old sister, Ana, under his protection. Ana was jilted by her sweetheart only hours before.

(I'll include similar examples from this same scene shortcut throughout this chapter.)

What Needs to Happen

Calder and the boy return to their hotel room and find that Ana has made a drastic change to her appearance: She has chopped her hair very short. Alexis doesn't want to see this. Ana says that the guard, Ilya, told her she was beautiful even with no hair, but he was lying. She feels foolish and ashamed, but Calder comforts her in her despair, a hint of his growing feelings for her. Alexis joins them.

I set down the basics of the scene: the goal (Calder wants to comfort Ana), the conflict (he can't suddenly make her happy), what is unresolved (he has secret feelings for her). By the way, in this "what needs to happen" paragraph, don't just list external actions; include things that happen to your characters internally as well. Here are examples of physical as well as internal actions for four fictional scenes:

Physical Actions	Internal Actions
Hero breaks into safe	Hero feels empathy for lawyer
Villain shoots his own son	Villain is scared for the first time

| The doctor meets new nurse | The doctor decides to cheat |
| The love interest walks out | The love interest loses hope |

For the scene outline, list what is essential to the scene at hand. Leave this scene outline paragraph in regular type font.

Recommended Reading

- *The First Five Pages: A Writer's Guide to Staying Out of the Rejection Pile* by Noah Lukeman: Chapters six through ten on the topic of dialogue.

- *Stein on Writing* by Sol Stein: Chapter seventeen on putting the senses into your writing.

- *Writing Down the Bones: Freeing the Writer Within* by Natalie Goldberg: Raises your heartstorming skills.

STEP II: THE DIALOGUE

Before we go to into the second part of the exercise, let's quickly look at the basics of writing dialogue. Dialogue, what the characters say to each other in a novel, can give a scene some of the essentials it needs. Dialogue can help with character development, deliver new information, and create tension. Some writers believe great dialogue should be a chain of poetic or comic gems, zingers, or brilliantly crafted one-liners. Some believe it should be exactly like everyday speech, like ordinary conversations you'd hear in a grocery store or at the Laundromat. But I believe great dialogue is a mixture of the two. It should sound real, but better. You want to believe the characters would actually come up with these words, but you also want the reader to secretly think, "I wish I talked like that."

Two exercises work for me when I write dialogue. One is to distill what needs to be said into a concise set of lines; the other is to transform normal lines into character-specific lines.

Distillation

Write out what has to be communicated—let's say a man needs to let his boss know that he'll do what he's told and be a good sport about it even if he'd rather not. Then cut it down into a smaller number of words that hold the same information. Packed tighter, the words will be more powerful. The story usually benefits from succinct, punchy dialogue. Boiling down what needs to be said forces you to think about the dialogue. It's not something you dash off. Distilling the dialogue helps you make sure that there is a purpose for this particular exchange. Dialogue is as important as any action sequence or bit of poetic description. What could be more useful than refining the language of your characters? It's how they will become real for the readers.

Here is an example of before and after dialogue distillation:

Undistilled Dialogue

Boss: I have a job for you. Take this package to Stephano's.
Henchman: What is it?
Boss: Why? You getting particular? Did you grow a conscience all of a sudden?
Henchman: I didn't say I wouldn't do it.
Boss: You make a thousand a week for a couple hours' work. You got a problem with that?
Henchman: I'm not complaining.
Boss: You didn't used to care what you were delivering.
Henchman: Gimme the package. I'll do it. Gotta pay my wife's credit card bills.

Distilled Dialogue

Boss: Take this package to Stephano's. What? You got a problem making money now?
Henchman: Baby always needs a new pair of shoes.

Of course, dialogue does not always need to be short. Don't be fooled if you find a long passage of dialogue in a great novel. It may still be very carefully chosen, edited, refined. Sometimes it takes a lot of rewriting for dialogue to sound spontaneous and natural. In long, well-written passages of dialogue, every phrase has a purpose and is spoken in a very particular order. If you have a scene with lots of dialogue, look at each line and ask:

1. What do we learn?

2. What is the goal?

3. What is the conflict?

4. Does the other character misinterpret anything in this line?

5. What is left unspoken?

6. What is left unresolved?

7. Does it fit my character?

Character-Specific Dialogue

To best know how to make your dialogue specific, ask yourself these questions about your main characters:

1. Is he a man of few words or talkative?

2. Does she mask her feelings, or does she wear her heart on her sleeve?

3. Is he casual or formal?

4. Is she modern or old-fashioned in her style?

5. Is he into a certain kind of slang because of a hobby or obsession? (Does he use golf lingo? Quote from *Monty Python* incessantly?)

6. Is she confident or nervous?

7. Is he optimistic or pessimistic?

8. Does she have a particular speech pattern? (Is she speaking in her native tongue or a second language? Does she have a speech impediment?)

9. Is he diplomatic and bureaucratic when he forms sentences, or is he more straightforward?

10. Does she have a sense of humor?

11. Does he come from a place where people talk in a distinct way?

12. Does she come from a time in history when people talked in a distinct way?

Characters are more fun to listen to when they speak differently from one another. And stories are easier to follow when the characters are easy to identify and remember by the way they speak. Now that you know your main characters well, make sure their dialogue is character specific.

For example, here is a passage of dialogue between the sardonic valet Jeeves and his colorful master, Bertie Wooster, from P.G. Wodehouse's *Jeeves in the Morning*. First the boring mock version I made up, and then the real version, steeped in character.

Nonspecific Mock Version

Wooster: We're in trouble.
Jeeves: What's the matter, sir?

Wooster: There's a disaster on the way.
Jeeves: Is that right, sir?

Real, Character-Specific Version

Wooster: Here's a nice state of things!
Jeeves: Sir?
Wooster: Hell's foundations have been
quivering.
Jeeves: Indeed, sir?

In the real version, we get a sense of the location and period in history (England in the 1920s) from, among other things, the phrase "nice state of things." The relationship between the two characters is clear, even in this short exchange. Wooster involves his manservant in his daily trials, and Jeeves is a patient listener. We also understand a lot about their personalities. From the fact that Wooster exaggerates and yet remains basically lighthearted about his troubles, we discern that he is a silly but likable fellow. Because of Jeeves's frugality with words we take him to be a man who thinks more than he speaks. The phrase "Indeed, sir" in response to an impending disaster so huge it rocks the underworld paints the portrait of a superhumanly calm caretaker.

When you write dialogue, show off your characters' personalities with word choices, profanity, slang, verbosity, or silence—whatever lets them shine through strongest.

My writer sister, Cynthia, teaches her screenwriting students about the "A, B, and C choices in dialogue" that she developed from listening to actors talk about their craft.

The A choice is the normal (boring) take on the line of dialogue. The B choice is less cliché. The C choice is even more interesting and original. People tend to say things like, "What time is it?" in similar ways, but they say things like, "I love you" or "that scared me" or "I'm attracted to her" in character-specific ways, depending on their personalities, geographic locations, and periods of history. You'll know instinctually which lines of dialogue should be written more character specific than others.

Take a look at the following examples. I'm sure you'll be able to pick the memorable line from each of these classics.

From *Casablanca*:

- **A choice:** Let's toast to our future.

- **B choice:** I can't keep my eyes off of you. Here's to us.

- **C choice:** Here's looking at you, Kid.

From *Gone With the Wind*:

- **A choice:** You've killed my love for you. I wash my hands of the whole situation.

- **B choice:** Figure it out yourself. I've had enough.

- **C choice:** Frankly, my dear, I don't give a damn.

Shortcut to the Scene: Dialogue Exercise

In the second part of the "Shortcut to the Scene" exercise, sketch out your best guess as to what dialogue will be in the scene. If you're like me, you hear and see many of your scenes before you write them. So you may already know what you want your characters to say word for word. If not, just write down what needs to be said or communicated. You can distill it and make it more character specific in Step IV of the exercise.

When I start writing dialogue in the first draft of a scene, I can get carried away and write only dialogue, forgetting to include action or reflection. Or sometimes I am so determined not to forget the next clever line of dialogue that just occurred to me that I rush through the other parts of the scene, short-changing my descriptions of internal reactions. Outlining my dialogue in advance reassures me that I have a plan set up that I already like and that is easy to read.

Type the lines of dialogue justified to the left with only the speaker's name in front of it—no "he said," "she said." You can even use the character's initial to save time.

Not this:

> "Tell me, Nathanial," said Jessica. "Do you still think of me?"

Just this:

> J: Tell me, N. Do you still think of me?

Here is another example from the scene shortcut I wrote while working on *The Fetch*.

Projected Dialogue

Ana: He never loved me. When we got the measles and had to shave off our hair, Ilya

told me that I was still beautiful. I wanted
to believe everything he said, but he lied
to me.
Calder: I'll tell you the truth. (she's scared)
You are beautiful, with or without hair, and
you are worthy of the deepest love on earth
or in heaven. That's the truth.
Alexis: Better let me have a try.

I make the dialogue section bold so that it is easy to see at a glance in the middle of the page when the three parts of the exercise are eventually printed out together.

STEP III: THE TEN-MINUTE HEARTSTORM

Set a timer and write as fast as you can about the scene for ten minutes. This is your *heartstorm*. Don't overthink it. Don't think at all. Feel the scene, the emotions, the sensations, the wonder. Don't judge what comes out of you. Be bold and swift. Don't worry about typing mistakes or punctuation or tense or misspellings or fact-checking. Just think about the scene you're preparing. Think of the emotions involved, the smells, tastes, scents, textures, sounds. Think of the strangest details and how they affect the characters. Is there something in the setting that illustrates the theme of the novel? Look at the interaction of your characters from different angles. What's happening outside the window? In the next room? What are the characters thinking or feeling that they aren't saying? Let your mind go anywhere and everywhere, and write as fast as you can.

Again, here is an example from the same scene shortcut. I put several phrases in bold after I wrote the paragraph below because I thought they were the best, most useful bits. (You could also use a highlighter to mark your favorite phrases if that is easier for you to see, or if you would rather write long-hand instead of typing this exercise.) I actually incorporated ideas from the bits in bold, in one form or another, into the draft of my scene.

Ten-Minute Heartstorm

Her despair frightens Calder, because he doesn't think he has any control over it. She is white and trembling, **much like one of the ghosts from the Land of Lost Souls**. How can she not realize she's beautiful? It's a cramped, depressing cell of a washroom, reminiscent of the House of Special Purpose. He **gently herds** her away from the mirror, but in a respectful way, not a pushy way. He understands why Alexis can't stand to see her like this—it's heartbreaking. Calder makes sure she can't see herself, her reflection, anymore—it's not the real her. Calder sees her for her true soul—he wishes that this was what she could see in a looking glass. **Ana confesses in the little bathroom** almost like he really is **a priest** and she's a sinner. The scene stops **short of weeping** (more powerful to hold back here) he has to turn her face away from him, she is too dear to bear. He **grooms her with** the **familiarity** of a father. The release of emotion draws the boy in. There is a strange music sifting in from another part of the hotel—a violin or maybe **singing**. Could be a song Calder remembers from a past Death Scene, an Italian wedding. I don't know. Alexis brings **humor** and lightness into the space. Her tears dry. Calder and the boy have teamed up to ease her pain.

When you write a heartstorm, you will find that those best ideas you end up putting in bold would not have come to you if you hadn't traveled through the other ideas first.

Culling the Poetry

During the 1963 dedication of the Robert Frost Library at Amherst College, John F. Kennedy made these bold statements about poetry: "When power leads man to arrogance, poetry reminds him of his limitations. When power narrows the area of man's concern, poetry reminds him of the richness and diversity of his existence. When power corrupts, poetry cleanses."

Poetry has profound power. When you do the ten-minute heartstorm writing to get at the emotions, senses, details, resonance, and symbolism in your story, you are unearthing your personal poetry. When a passage in your novel is bland or cliché, poetry will bring color and originality. When a scene is harsh or sterile, your poetry will provide readers with grace and warmth to make the scene live in their imaginations. When your page is swimming in sentimental crap, your poetry will sharpen and defrock your prose, lifting each line toward truth.

The heartstorm part of this exercise may be new to you. If you're having trouble letting go and allowing your inner poet to babble on the topic of your scene, try this poetry exercise to warm up.

Take as long as you like (it doesn't need to be limited to ten minutes) and write a stream of consciousness page on something other than a scene from your novel. It doesn't matter what you write about—write anything. But try using a topic that holds emotion: what it's like waking up the morning after you've had your heart broken, the experience of seeing the ocean for the first time after growing up in the desert, recalling an embarrassing episode from junior high. Try to choose a powerful concept, then let your imagination run wild.

Afterward, highlight your favorite phrases. Even if you don't think there's anything worth keeping, choose ten or more phrases that you like. Start with your very favorites and work down. Then line them up like a poem; enhance the wording if you'd like. Then read it back as if it were composed as a poem.

Here's an example I created as a demonstration.

I used to have this recurring dream when I was a teenager and in my early twenties. Well, at least I had it three or four times. I'd dreamed I was running along the ground, a flat dry plain. The dirt was dark red, kind of like Arizona or Nevada, desert-ish, and there were huge, rectangular buttes as high as office buildings the same color as the ground. These are the kind of blocks of stone I imagine when someone tells that illustration of "infinite time"—if a bird came and pecked a single time at a huge block of stone once every hundred years, in the time it would take to wear that stone down to nothing, that's infinity. That kind of enormous, hard block. There are almost no plants in this place—a few dry shrubs and maybe a dead tree in the distance like a silhouette. There is no animal life that I can see except a couple of dark, sharp-edged birds in the sky, ones with pointy, angled wings like albatross. The light is coming from the lower half of the sky, as if it's after-noon or early morning, but the clouds are so solid and dense that the light's muted and diffused. I am running so hard I am tilt-ing forward, but I have my head turned to the side toward the light as if something is going to happen there. Here is the most interesting and frightening thing about the dream. I know I am on another planet. The reason I know this is because the horizon is excruciatingly flat. When we see a broad horizon on earth, we think it looks straight, or flat, but we're actually seeing the slight curve of the planet. Here, in this alien place, the horizon is so flat it is almost lifting at each side, going concave. It's so flat I feel like someone shrank me to the size of a tiny mouse. It's so flat that this planet, whatever it is, must be a hundred times bigger than earth. And then here's the loneliest part of the dream, the fact that time seems to have slowed way down. Because I'm running so fast I'm leaning forward, and at the same time I'm not getting anywhere very fast. I wear a long, old coat like a western riding coat split up the back. The wind whips at me and the coattails flap. But I keep trying to run, keep looking at the horizon, keep waiting for something to happen and feeling diminished by the immensity of this planet that I don't know the name of.

Here's the poem, distilled from the page of writing:

> I dream I am running
> The dirt, dark red
> Huge buttes as high as office buildings

Dry shrubs, a dead tree in the distance
Sharp-edged birds
The lower half of the sky, muted and diffused
I am running, tilting forward
The horizon is excruciatingly flat
So flat, it is lifting
So flat, I'm a mouse
So flat, this planet must be a hundred times
        bigger than Earth
The loneliest part
Time seems to have slowed
I keep running, looking at the horizon
Diminished
Waiting for something to happen

The resulting "poem" is no masterpiece, but the babbling of the "say anything" page could be distilled into some concise imagery. If the heartstorm part of the "Shortcut to the Scene" exercise isn't working for you at first, start by warming up with this poetry exercise before you move to a ten-minute heartstorm on your actual scene.

If you try the "Shortcut to the Scene" exercise and it does not pan out, rethink to make sure you aren't trying to make a scene out of something that should be summarized or cut from the book completely.

Fun Stuff

- Go to a live performance of anything (music, dance, drama, puppets, drumming, anything) and just soak it in.

- Take a scene you've already written but with which you are not thrilled, print out a copy, tear it into small pieces, shuffle the scraps, and then try to piece it back together. Seeing the words that make up the scene jumbled and lost can be very freeing.

STEP IV: PUTTING IT TOGETHER

Once you're ready for this final step, print out the three earlier steps of this exercise with the "what needs to happen" paragraph at the top, the "projected dialogue" in the middle, and the "ten-minute heartstorm" material at the bottom. You want it on one page so you can refer to it easily. Now, lay this page next to your keyboard as you write the actual scene.

For me, this page acts as a menu. I order something from one of the three parts to open the scene. It might be a simple piece of action from part one, then the first line of dialogue, then some bit of reflection or description touched on in my heartstorm. I gather the pieces I need to form the chain of moments in my scene not from the air or my memory, but from a plan that I already have printed out and ready. Without using the "Shortcut to the Scene" exercise, winging it from an ordinary outline, the scene from *The Fetch* might have come out something like this on the first try:

> When they came back to the hotel, they found Ana standing in the washroom, her hair cut off in a jagged mess and a pair of scissors still in her hands. The sink held a pile of gold fluff. She was pale, staring at herself in the mirror. The boy turned away and sat on the bed without speaking to her, but Calder brought her a chair. She let herself be seated. Calder slipped the rusty sheers out of her hand, wishing he could remove her pain as easily.
>
> "Ilya never loved me," she said. "He saw a photograph of me, after we'd shaved our heads when we were ill. He said I was still pretty. He said a lot of things, but he lied."
>
> "He wasn't lying about that," said Calder. "Of course you're pretty. You're beautiful."
>
> At this she began to weep, and Calder stood behind her and began to snip at her locks, trying to even out the places where

she had cut the most unevenly. Her tears
slowed.

"Here, let me do that," said Alexis. He
stood in the washroom doorway now.

"Can you do better?" asked Calder.

"I can try." The boy took over as his sister's barber.

Music sifted in from another room in the
hotel, a slow and scratchy waltz.

By the time Calder had gathered the
discarded tresses into the rubbish can, Ana
was smiling. But when she looked at herself
in the mirror, she gasped.

What's wrong with this version? It's underwritten, not emotional enough. It skims over the passion. Not enough detail.
Too "on the nose." Not original enough—people say and do
the expected. Without the shortcut exercise I would have
probably rewritten it two or three more times before it came
out as good as the first draft did using the exercise. Instead, I
was able to write the following actual first draft of the scene:

When they came to the hotel room door, it
was unlocked. Alexis opened it wide without hesitation—Calder would have knocked.
But a moment later, the boy turned away
from whatever he had seen and walked to
the small table in the corner where he sat
looking at the wall. Calder saw then what
had made him go pale. Ana stood before

the washroom mirror, leaning on the sink. A familiar sight was there, a bird's nest of hair filling the basin.

She had cropped her golden hair as close to her head as Calder had cut his, and not at all neater. She stared at her reflection, trembling and blanched. The sight of this made Calder dizzy for a moment, the idea she might be struggling with despair the way a ghost might. He took a chair from beside the little table, brought it to Ana, and gently lowered her into it. She let herself be seated, rested her hands in her lap, a rusty pair of sheers still hooked in her fingers. Calder closed the washroom door most of the way, to keep the boy from hearing them, but not all the way, for the sake of propriety.

Sitting now, no longer able to see her reflection, Ana looked up at Calder with wide eyes.

"He never loved me."

Slowly Calder took the scissors from her and set them in the sink.

"When we caught the measles," she said, "and had to shave off our hair, Ilya saw the photographs and told me that I was still beautiful." She felt the back of her head. "I wanted to believe everything he said, but he lied to me."

Calder lowered himself to one knee beside her and asked, "If I speak plainly, will you listen to me?" He saw fear flash behind her eyes, but she nodded consent. "I'm not going to lie to you," he warned. He could see Ana steel herself for whatever was coming next. She took a deep breath and looked him in the eyes.

"You are beautiful," he said. "With or without hair, and you are worthy of the deepest love on earth or in heaven."

She shuddered and tears welled into her eyes. He took her gently by the shoulders and turned her away from him. Then he took the scissors from the bed of hair in the sink and tilted her head forward as he snipped at her ravaged locks, trying to even out the places where she had cut the most unevenly.

"Hopeless job," said Alexis. He stood in the washroom doorway, shaking his head.

"Can you do better?" asked Calder.

"Judging from your own head, yes." The boy took over as his sister's barber, brushing the loose hairs from her shoulders and draping one of the hotel's threadbare towels around her neck.

Somewhere in another hotel room two voices began to sing, faltered, laughed, be-

gan again in a rustic harmony, Italian perhaps, though the lyrics were too muffled to
make out.

Ana's tears dried on her face, and by the
time Alexis was finished, and Calder had
gathered the discarded tresses into the rubbish can, she was smiling. When she stood
up and looked at herself in the mirror, she
gave a start. "Oh, my ..."

Now let's take a quick look at how this scene benefited from
the ten-minute heartstorm portion of this exercise. For instance, the phrases from the heartstorm that I highlighted as
favorites influenced the final scene as follows:

1. **much like one of the ghosts from the Land of
   Lost Souls:** The sight of this made Calder dizzy
   for a moment, the idea she might be struggling
   with despair the way a ghost might.

2. **gently herds:** gently lowered her into (the chair).
   She let herself be seated.

3. **Ana confesses in the little bathroom/a priest/a
   sinner:** Calder closed the washroom door most of
   the way, to keep the boy from hearing them, but
   not all the way, for the sake of propriety.

4. **short of weeping:** She shuddered and tears welled
   into her eyes. He took her gently by the shoulders
   and turned her away from him.

5. **grooms her with … familiarity:** tilted her head forward …

6. **singing:** two voices began to sing, faltered, laughed, began again in a rustic harmony, Italian perhaps, though the lyrics were too muffled to make out.

7. **humor:** "Hopeless job," said Alexis.

The first draft of the scene changed very little before it was published because I had jumped forward at least three rewrites by using this shortcut. And I found that I wrote about three times faster, too. The difference was that I wasn't all in my left brain—organized but lacking magic/emotion/ beauty—and I wasn't all in my right brain—waxing poetic but all over the place. I knew I had already set down some of each in the exercise, and it was clearly laid out, at hand, as a reference while I composed. And it wasn't someone else's advice or rules lying there beside my keyboard, needing to be translated in order to be useful—it was all me.

○ ● ○

John Kenneth Galbraith once said, "There are days when the result is so bad that no fewer than five revisions are required. In contrast, when I'm greatly inspired, only four revisions are needed." Even with all these shortcuts, there *will* be rewriting. I'm simply trying to help you get at your deeper draft faster. If it takes ten drafts to get it good enough to send to your agent, and drafts one to three are frustrating, and draft four is when it begins to shine for you and get exciting, know that what

I'm trying to do in this book is help you get that fourth-draft glow the first time through.

Of all the tricks I came up with while struggling to find time-savers for my second novel, the "Shortcut to the Scene" has been the most successful for me. Before I started using it, it took me all afternoon to write the first draft of one scene. After discovering the technique, in the same five hours I could write three.

CHAPTER 5

BALANCING SCENE, SUMMARY, AND REFLECTION

*A manuscript is such a tricky, delicate thing: Even if
everything else is perfect, it must not be too slow or too fast.*

—Noah Lukeman

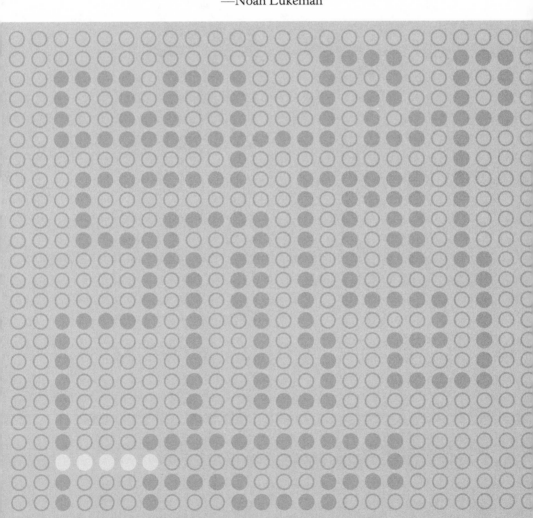

In addition to realizing the core of your story, discovering the right storytelling device, and knowing where the crosshairs moments are, it's also important to find a balance between the parts of the story that would be best played out in scenes and the parts that should be summarized, made into reflection, or cut altogether. Realizing this before you start writing your draft not only saves you time, it helps to keep your writing alive and flowing.

First, it's important to understand the difference between a scene and summary. Scenes are those places where the plot slows down and happens in real time so the readers can see and hear the action as if it were happening in the same room with them. Those parts of the story are where characters reveal themselves and where things change. Summary, on the other hand, is used to give readers a shortened version of the action and should contain information the readers need to know for the scenes to make sense. (As my sister would say, summary is when someone tells you about going on a date. A scene is when you get to go on the date with him.) Reflective passages, then, are the places where the author steps out of the action and makes an observation that somehow enriches the story.

For example, when you write two pages of dialogue that takes place in the getaway car while your kidnappers argue and then write two sentences on the four-hour police investigation following the disappearance of the victim, you have followed a scene with summary. When you write the detailed actions that take place in the ER as a character takes in her final breath, then follow it with half a page comparing death with the onset of winter, you have followed a scene with reflection.

THE SCENE

How will you know which parts of your story are best told as scenes? Most of the time it's obvious. You feel it. Those parts play over and over again in your head like scenes from a play or movie, or like a memory from your own life. As we discussed in chapter four, a scene takes place in real time; has a beginning, a middle, and an end; has a goal; creates tension; and moves the story along. When you write your outline of the novel, do you find yourself describing some sections in so much detail that you've written in lines of dialogue? Smells like a scene to me.

SUMMARY

If the readers need to know how you got from point A to point B, but nothing of deep significance happens during that passage, you might summarize it—that is, describe the action out of real time. But look carefully to make sure a summary is even necessary. If George was at home and shows up at the theater, and you've skipped the trip uptown, the reader will assume you did so because the drive was not important.

If you find that your summary is running long, look back. Perhaps it's meant to be a scene. You don't want the narration of your novel to sound like a detailed outline. Would part of the summarized action be dynamic enough to open up into a scene? If so, get in there and write the dialogue, the details, the stuff that made it too interesting to skim over.

Scene	Summary (or Cut)
Toby decodes a message	Toby drives to the library, browses the Web, misinterprets code seventeen times
Bea falls in love with the doctor	Bea kills time in the waiting room before meeting the doctor
Max reads a DNA report and realizes he's related to the villain	Max wakes up in the morning, puts on his slippers, and makes coffee before looking at the e-mail that includes the test results

Here's what it would sound like if this well-written passage from the short story "Don't Look Now," in the collection *Don't Look Now* by Daphne du Maurier, were interrupted by a piece of unnecessary summary. (The bold type indicates the fictional summary.)

"Well, this decides it, doesn't it?" she said. "Here is the proof. We have to leave Venice because we're going home. It's Johnnie

who's in danger, not us. This is what Christine
was trying to tell the twins."

They readied themselves for bed. John
read the newspaper he had found in the
lobby. Laura watched the night sky through
the uncurtained windows. They switched
off the light at midnight without a dozen
words passing between them, slept calmly,
and woke at dawn almost in the same instant, or so it seemed to him.

The first thing John did the following
morning was to put a call through to the
headmaster at the preparatory school.

Nothing happened during the night that would warrant men-
tioning it, which is why du Maurier skipped it.

Here is an example of summary that should be a scene, and
was a scene in the real version of this passage from *Their Eyes
Were Watching God* by Zora Neale Hurston. (The bold type
indicates the fictional summarizing of the missing scene.)

She saw him coming from the outhouse with
a queer loping gait, swinging his head from
side to side and his jaws clenched in a funny
way. **There was nothing she could do. He was
a mad man, and she was glad she had left
two empty chambers in the gun so she had
time to load the rifle before he had time to
kill her. She brought him down, but in the
struggle Tea Cake still managed to bite her.**

> Janie pried the dead Tea Cake's teeth from her
> arm. It was the meanest moment of eternity.

The death of Tea Cake is far too dramatic and emotional, far too pivotal, to be summarized.

In this passage from Carson McCullers's *The Member of the Wedding,* we go from a scene in a hotel room to a scene at Frankie's (F. Jasmine's) home with the trek between summarized perfectly.

> F. Jasmine told herself: Get out! And after
> first starting toward the door, she turned and
> climbed out on the fire-escape and quickly
> reached the alley ground.
>
> She ran like a chased person fleeing from
> the crazy-house at Milledgeville, looking
> neither to the right nor left, and when she
> reached the corner of her own home block,
> she was glad to see John Henry West. He was
> looking for bats around the street light, and
> the familiar sight of him calmed her a little.
>
> "Uncle Royal has been calling you," he said.

McCullers gives us just enough information. We see how Frankie escaped and feel the emotions involved. And the summary took her less than a hundred words.

Tips for Writing Summary

Writing summary does not mean starting at the moment the last scene ended and covering everything that happens up to the moment the next scene begins. You only need to include those things that are significant to the storytelling. There is a lot the readers will assume.

Things you don't need:

1. **Uneventful travel.** People walking out of rooms or riding, walking, or flying to a new location. Unless there's something important about the way they get to the next place, leave it out.

2. **Home-life maintenance.** If you don't say what happened the rest of the night, readers will assume that normal things took place: sleeping, reading, watching television.

3. **Workday maintenance.** We know that the lawyer will probably have meetings, take phone calls, read briefs. We'll assume the teacher will give lessons, grade papers, have coffee in the staff lounge. No need to even skim over that stuff unless doing so helps your story.

4. **Relationship maintenance.** If you skip how your hero kisses his wife and kids when he gets home, what he says to them, and the look on this face during dinner, readers will assume that his relationships are rolling along as before.

5. **Ongoing emotions already stated.** If you describe your protagonist being depressed and skip telling us her frame of mind between breakfast and dinner, readers will assume she continued to act

depressed. No need to repeat or fortify this idea unless it helps the story.

Where should you start your summary? If the next important thing that happens after the last scene is your villain seeing the hero's wife grocery shopping two weeks later, don't start with the villain deciding to visit the market or with him parking his car. Start with him seeing the wife and what that moment means.

What makes great summary? You hear only what you need to hear and with only the most relevant details. And you hear these things in the style and tone of the whole story. Here is an example from John Steinbeck's *The Grapes of Wrath*:

> Ma passed the boiled potatoes out and brought the half sack from the tent and put it with the pan of pork. The family ate standing, shuffling their feet and tossing the hot potatoes from hand to hand until they cooled.
>
> Ma went to the Wilson tent and stayed for ten minutes, and then she came out quietly. "It's time to go," she said.
>
> The men went under the tarpaulin. Granma still slept, her mouth wide open. They lifted the whole mattress gently and passed it up on top of the truck. Granma drew up her skinny legs and frowned in her sleep, but she did not awaken.
>
> Uncle John and Pa tied the tarpaulin over the crosspiece, making a little tight tent on

top of the load. They lashed it down to the side-bars. And then they were ready.

We only needed to feel what it was like to be the Joads during this last hour before they left the camp. We didn't need it to be written out like a scene where we heard all the dialogue. We didn't need to hear anyone's words except Ma's. We didn't need to go into the Wilson tent or hear a blow-by-blow description of the men deciding how best to move the old woman. Those 140 words painted the whole picture and took us from the beginning of the meal to the moments before their departure.

Summary Exercise

Take a year of your life and try summarizing it into one paragraph. See if you can find the most significant aspects to highlight. What changed that year? What would someone need to know in order for the next year of your life to make sense? Read it to someone else and see if they get a sense of that shortened journey through time. If you have trouble with a year of your own life, try summarizing a year of someone else's life, a season of your favorite TV drama or comedy, a season for your favorite sports team. Repeat until ease sets in.

REFLECTION

Perhaps you feel a scene should be cut, but skipping to the next significant piece of action feels incomplete. Depending on your writing style and narrating voice, you may want to replace the scene with reflection.

What makes great reflection? It's a passage of writing that pulls the readers out of the word-by-word, step-by-step, description of actions and conversations and takes them to a place outside of time and space. Reflection draws significance out of the story, reflects on the attitudes of the characters, or opens up another level of understanding about the history or culture in the story. It may add new depth to one or more characters' behavior or philosophies, give insight into some piece of backstory, or make connections between previously unrelated facts from the text. The best reflective passages are profound, poetic, humorous, charming, or chilling, depending on the type of novel.

Here is a great example of reflection from Milan Kundera's *The Unbearable Lightness of Being.*

> The heavier the burden, the closer our lives come to the earth, the more real and truthful they become.
>
> Conversely, the absolute absence of a burden causes man to be lighter than air, to soar into the heights, take leave of the earth and his earthly being, and become only half real, his movements as free as they are insignificant.
>
> What then shall we choose? Weight or lightness?

Good reflection offers up images and ideas that illustrate the struggles and paradoxes that the story holds. Use it carefully.

Reflection is like a spice you add to your food. Just enough of the right flavor is wonderful; too much or the wrong flavor ruins it.

If the ethnic background and cultural style of your Korean protagonist's childhood has an impact on his thoughts, feelings, and actions, you might write a reflective passage giving the readers a feel for this culture. If the readers need to get a sense of the social norms during the Roaring Twenties, you might write a reflective passage on that period of history, giving them a flavor of the story's setting in time. Reflection can also do everything from illustrate themes and provide character sketches to emphasize irony, make analogies, enhance foreshadowing, poetically tie together two or more seemingly unrelated storylines … I'm getting carried away, but you see that the possibilities are vast.

Deciding when and how to use reflection is an individual writer's choice. The reflection has to fit in with the tone and style of your narration or come from the first-person narrator's natural speech and thought patterns. If you find that the reflection you are composing feels forced or too poetic, take a step back. Perhaps the passage is not needed. There's nothing worse than bad (pompous, sappy, or boring) reflection. Sleep on it. Come back to it fresh in the morning and see if it begins to flow better.

Here are examples of reflection being used in various ways.

Reflecting on the Themes or Major Conflicts in the Story

The thing about having it all is, it should include having the *ability* to have it all. Maybe there are some people who know how to have it all. They're probably off in a group somewhere, laughing at those of us who have it all but don't know how to.

—*Postcards from the Edge*
by Carrie Fisher

On the cover that leaned against the dirty couch, John and Yoko pressed together in a kiss they would never finish. People were always trashing Yoko Ono, blaming her for breaking up the Beatles, but Josie knew they were just jealous that John preferred Yoko to some bloated megaband. Nobody ever really loved a lover. Because love was a private party, and nobody got on the guest list.

—*Paint It Black* by Janet Fitch

In both these cases the authors capsulize the story struggle using the language and personality of their main characters: Fisher's protagonist is lost and overwhelmed; she feels like an outsider and searches for answers but with a sense of humor. Fitch's protagonist is grieving the death of her lover; she feels that no one understood their relationship, especially her lover's mother, who blames Josie for the young man's suicide, thus her sympathy for Yoko's bad rap. In only one paragraph these passages each say a lot about the character and the story in general, and are entertaining to boot.

Reflecting on a Character's Personality

I don't know why it should be, I am sure, but the sight of another man asleep when I am up maddens me. It seems to me so shocking to see the precious hours of a man's life—the priceless moments that will never come back to him again—being wasted in mere brutish sleep.

—*Three Men in a Boat*
by Jerome K. Jerome

Here the author gives us some insight into the main character's personality by having that character reflect on something he feels strongly about but that is unusual. Being annoyed by a fellow human being's sleep, and feeling comfortable enough to admit it, says a lot about the protagonist.

Reflecting on a Character's Thoughts

Life's sounds all rang with a curious lightness and flatness, as if a resonating base beneath them had been removed. They told Clarence Wilmot what he had long suspected, that the universe was utterly indifferent to his states of mind and as empty of divine content as a corroded kettle.

—*In the Beauty of the Lilies*
by John Updike

In this case, the author reflects on the character's thoughts and feelings, summing up his state of mind, by translating something simple (the small everyday sounds he hears around him) into a kind of philosophical realization about something huge (that there is no God).

Reflecting on and Recapping a Segment of Time

For three astonishing years she had lived and prayed from the inside of a kaleidoscope. Everything fit into a design of feeling, a pattern linking all souls and minds together. She felt God's presence in the design, and nothing seemed out of place. Every person was like a piece of glass in a giant rose window. Now the pattern was gone.
—*Lying Awake* by Mark Salzman

Here the author doesn't just say that three years passed, doesn't merely summarize the years (she worked here, did these activities, retained these habits); he adds meaning and beauty to that summarized piece of the protagonist's life by creating a metaphor, an easy way for readers to picture what was significant in those years and how they brought her to the present.

Reflecting Back on the Whole Story

She thought of all the people in all the paintings she had seen that day, not just Father's, in all the paintings of the world, in fact. Their eyes, the particular turn of a head, their loneliness or suffering or grief was borrowed by

an artist to be seen by other people throughout the years who would never see them
face to face. People who would be that close
to her, she thought, a matter of a few arms'
lengths, looking, looking, and they would
never know her.

—*Girl in Hyacinth Blue*
by Susan Vreeland

Here the author uses the character's thoughts at the close of
the book, written in such a way that those ideas not only describe the moment—the character contemplating the strange
path of communication in art from model to artist to art observer—but also describe the whole story, or set of stories—
different people from varied countries, situations, and periods
of history, moved by the same painting.

Tips for Writing Reflection

Reflection shouldn't distract your readers. It should fit seam-
lessly into the text, be purposeful, and be easily grasped.

1. **Only write reflection in the first place if it fits
   your style.** Some gritty action novels have none.
   Some old-fashioned romances have tons. There's
   no rule, but it should feel natural.

2. **The passage of reflection needs to serve a purpose.** It's not there just to sound interesting or pretty.
   What do the readers learn from it? It either tells them
   something about the character, about the setting

in culture and history, about the theme, or about the plot (foreshadowing or looking back). After you compose your passage of reflection, look at it again. Review the list of examples above. Does your reflective passage enlighten the readers about the central struggle in the novel? Or does it let them in to the protagonist's personality or thoughts? Does it replace a summary with a more profound illustration of skipped time? Is it a closing passage that looks back on and draws meaning from the whole story?

3. **It should fit in perfectly with the language of the scenes and passages surrounding it.** Be careful not to include reflection that sounds like a different writer was hired to add it.

4. **Don't be too obvious.** Nothing is easier to ridicule than corny reflection. *His life had been an open book, she the pen, and his sweat and tears the ink with which she composed a letter of regret.* (Okay, I made that up, but you get the idea. Unless you're writing a comedy and are even sillier than me, cut the cliché-laden reflection.)

5. **Be clear.** There's no point in having a purpose in mind if it's too obtuse for the readers to understand.

Reflection Exercise

Look at the list of reflection examples and choose one type (story struggle, protagonist's personality, protagonist's thoughts, recapping time, reflecting on the whole story) and have the protagonist or narrator in your novel reflect appropriately. No blow-by-blow action—that would be the description part of a regular scene. No simple skimming over the plot—that would be summary. Have your character or narrator contemplate another character's intentions, ruminate on a problem, muse on a concept—whatever fits your character's personality the best. This passage may never end up in the manuscript, but it will help you warm up to writing reflection.

○ ● ○

Scene, summary, and reflection aren't all black and white—sometimes a scene will have a sentence or two of summary imbedded in it, or a summary might lapse into reflection, or a first-person narrator might throw in a bit of reflection during a scene he is describing. Your choices as a writer will become natural as your style matures.

Recommended Reading

- *On Writing Well* by William K. Zinsser: Part II, "Methods"

- *The 38 Most Common Fiction Writing Mistakes* by Jack M. Bickham: Chapter six, "Don't Describe Sunsets"

- *The Writer's Digest Handbook of Novel Writing*: "Scene and Sequel: The Two Keys to Strong Plots" by Jack M. Bickham

FINDING YOUR RHYTHM: WHAT AFFECTS BALANCE

When my nephew was small, perhaps five years old, I stood on the porch steps watching him struggle with his bike that had been stripped of its training wheels. By chance I witnessed the moment he learned how to balance as he made a turn, that combination of speed, gravity, and coordination that so soon becomes instinctual. His brief look of surprise was in one heartbeat replaced with delight as he began to ride around and around, banking into a tight turn and straightening without even touching his sneaker to the pavement.

Somewhere during the writing of *A Certain Slant of Light* I experienced something akin to this. I learned my own personal balance between scene, summary, and reflection. I took a small and mysterious step up the skill ladder, big enough to get published.

The rhythm between scene, summary, and reflection may depend on and be guided by many things: genre, characters, setting, plot, themes, and your writing style. That's why finding the balance is so personal.

• **Genre.** Recently I started wondering about other authors' scene-to-summary-to-reflection balance, so flipped open a variety of novels and took some notes. In the first fifteen pages the books varied drastically in their patterns, but I noticed some trends: Commercial novels (such as Elmore Leonard's *Get Shorty* and Peter Blauner's *Man of the Hour*) and young adult novels (like Margaret Craven's *I Heard the Owl Call My Name*) tended to have a higher percentage of scene—Leonard and Craven had around 70 percent and Blauner pretty much 100 percent. The literary novels had a higher percentage of reflection and summary—*One Hundred Years of Solitude* by Gabriel García Márquez had 80 percent reflection and summary, and *The Unbearable Lightness of Being* by Milan Kundera had almost 100 percent.

Although I found this interesting, there's no need for you to be bound by the genre in which you're writing. Do what feels natural to you, what works best for your story. But if you think you're writing a literary novel, and you tend to write lots of short scenes and almost no reflection, you might actually be writing commercial fiction. There's no sin in that. Be open-minded.

• **Character.** Your characters can affect how you use summary. Some of them require more backstory than others; so those novels will contain more summary. Some characters who are first-person narrators, by nature, will give you more passages of reflection. It depends on the personality of that character. Do they philosophize? Or are they storytellers who simply summarize exposition?

• **Setting.** The setting may have an effect on your scene rhythm, as well. If the setting is a place that symbolizes some weighty piece of history (Gettysburg, the Tower of London) or a sacred place (Jerusalem, a cathedral), it may steer you toward more reflection. If the setting entails something repetitive (a factory assembly line, a schoolroom), then a certain amount of summary may feel natural.

• **Plot.** The plot, of course, will have an effect on the rhythm between your scenes, summary, and reflection. If for the first half of the book the protagonist is alone, perhaps lost in the desert, there will be few dialogue scenes, lots of detailed descriptions of a number of small things (the character's body, the weather, the sand), and probably plenty of summary and reflection. If your whole novel takes place in a small boat where four people are trapped for a day, you'll probably have long scenes of dialogue.

• **Theme.** Theme may have an effect on your scene-to-summary-to-reflection pattern. If your theme is "emotionally distant husbands drive wives mad," you may have long scenes with lots of dialogue, but one-sided: the woman trying to wake up her man. If your theme is "emotionally distant husbands drive wives into silence," you may have very little dialogue and plenty of reflection as the female narrator struggles internally. If your theme is "war is necessary and inevitable," or if it's "war is bad," you may have the same scene-to-non-scene pattern either way, but the theme "every man is an island" will tend to have more reflection and fewer scenes with dialogue than the theme "people need each other." You get the idea.

• **Style.** Your style of writing, of course, affects on your rhythm. It's all part of your voice. If you are a get-down-to-business type of writer, you will probably have less (or at least shorter) reflection and you'll summarize things briefly. Scenes will start with the first significant moment. No frills.

If you're a poetic writer, you may intersperse reflection as transition between scenes, and you may summarize in great detail. The more you write, the more your scene-to-summary balance will become natural.

Rhythm Exercises

To help you find your rhythm, try one of these suggestions:

- **List your scenes.** Using your outline, list all of your scenes, skipping a line between each. Then write down on the in-between line whether there needs to be any transition between the scenes. Can you just jump to the next scene? Then mark those scenes with a Y for "YES, I'm absolutely positive this part should be written as a scene," or an M for "MAYBE this needs to be a scene, maybe I should rethink it and turn it into a summary or a passage of reflection."

- **Compound scenes.** Search your outline for scenes that could be combined. Here's an example: You write a scene where your protagonist argues with her husband as he's leaving for work, then summarize her driving the kids to school, then write a scene where she gets her feelings hurt by her son as she drops him off at the curb. Maybe you could combine the things that need to happen in the story. The other car won't start, so she's got the kids and her husband squished into her car. She's arguing with her husband as she's trying to drive and can't pay attention to the children who are trying to get her attention. As she pulls up to the school, her son hurts her feelings on purpose as he's getting out of the car. Lots going on. Not boring. And now the argument with the husband is tied to the child hurting her feelings. Characters who are feeling more than one emotion at the same time are interesting, and scenes where more than one thing happens are dynamic. See if you have any short scenes that might benefit from coupling up.

- **Scan your favorite book.** Take a novel by your favorite writer, someone you would like to emulate, and flip through the first fifty pages, jotting down the length, number, and order of scenes, summaries, and passages of reflection. You might be surprised.

- **Read.** This sounds like a longcut rather than a shortcut, but it really is the best way to find your personal balance. Read the writers you admire. Soon their rhythm of scene to summary to reflection will sound and feel so natural, it will start to come through in your own writing.

Fun Stuff

- Write about yesterday in your life. First summarize it in a paragraph, then write the most interesting part of it out as a scene (at least one page), then write another paragraph philosophizing, ruminating, and reflecting on the meaning found in that day.

- Go out in the world and get a feel for your physical balance. Ride a skateboard, go surfing, walk a gymnast's beam, roller skate, ride your bike in figure eights.

CHAPTER 6

PLANNING YOUR PLOT

*Writing a novel is like heading out over the open
sea in a small boat. It helps if you have a plan
and a course laid out.*

—John Gardner

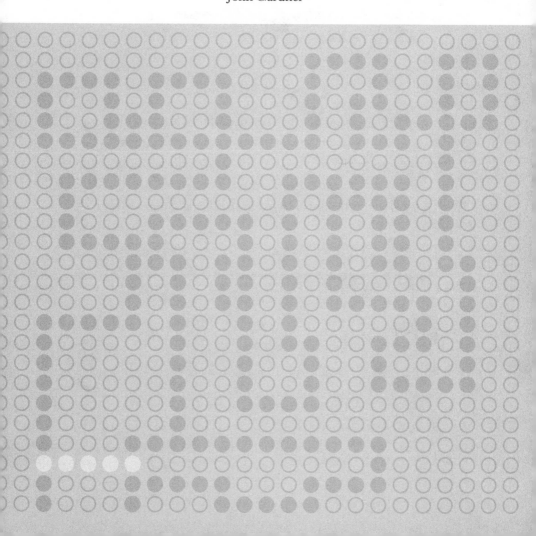

It's good to know where you're going. An outline helps you write a novel because it maps out where your turning points will be, how your setups and payoffs will work, and how you'll wrap up your subplots. (For tips on outlining, see chapter two of *Your First Novel*, by Ann Rittenberg and me.) But if you are one of those writers who does not want to be shackled with a traditional outline, you might find that one of the following techniques will speed up (and improve) your writing. And all of the following methods, by the way, can be used with an outline, as well.

Recommended Reading

- *The Writer's Journey: Mythic Structure for Storytellers and Screenwriters* by Christopher Vogler: An inspiring look at a story structure (inspired by Joseph Campbell) that is easy to picture and execute.

PLOT WEB

A plot web is a visual aid that reminds the writer of all the significant threads, from major plot points to subplots to tiny thematic details, that connect to a given character. While writing my first published novel, *A Certain Slant of Light*, I digressed from my usual habit and did not use an outline. But after I'd drafted about two hundred pages, at a point of plot complexity that overwhelmed me, I adopted two techniques for keeping my sanity and staying organized. The first was the plot web I created for both of my two main characters, Helen and James. I wrote their names in circles and drew lines outward from those circles, one for each topic that I needed to track for the character.

In this way, I didn't have to slow down to figure out if I'd missed a thread in the tapestry of the plot, and I didn't have to rewrite a scene as often to insert a missed subplot. I could glance up at my plot webs at the beginning of each scene.

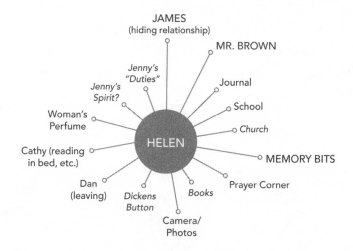

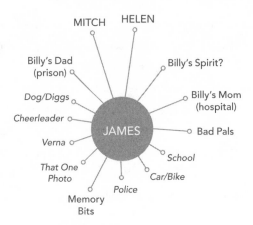

MITCH   HELEN

Billy's Dad
(prison)

Billy's Spirit?

Dog/Diggs

Billy's Mom
(hospital)

Cheerleader

Verna

JAMES

Bad Pals

That One
Photo

School

Police

Car/Bike

Memory
Bits

Let's look at some diagram illustrations for some well-known stories. For Jane Eyre, the writer is reminded to touch on the somewhat marginal character, Mrs. Poole, and include thoughts of Mr. Rochester's admirers. For Ebenezer Scrooge, the writer is reminded to insert the concept of charity and the subplot of those who are in debt to Scrooge. And for Bridget Jones, the writer is reminded to track the number of cigarettes smoked each day and to include Bridget's parents' marital woes.

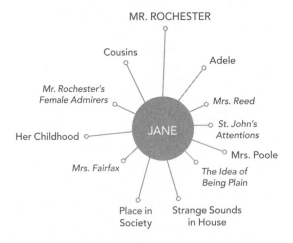

MR. ROCHESTER

Cousins

Adele

Mr. Rochester's
Female Admirers

Mrs. Reed

Her Childhood

JANE

St. John's
Attentions

Mrs. Poole

Mrs. Fairfax

The Idea of
Being Plain

Place in
Society

Strange Sounds
in House

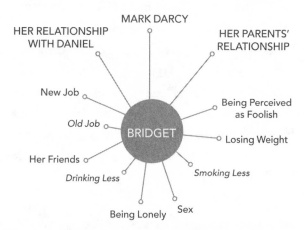

Pin your plot web diagrams to the wall near your computer. With them nearby, you can write freely without a blow-by-blow outline, but still be reminded of important subplots and themes.

I find it helpful to differentiate between major plot points, subplots, and details either by writing the major points in large print, the subplots in medium, and the details in small print (as shown), or by writing or highlighting the categories in different colored.

Fun Stuff

- As with the collage activity at the end of chapter one, go through magazines and the Web to find pictures that remind you of the pieces of the story puzzle that affect each of your main characters—the subplots, key emotions, etc. Write the character's name in the center of a blank page or small piece of tag board and glue the images around the name like the numbers on a clock. Put the character collages up where you can see them from your writing area. See if they don't help you track that character's hopes, fears, troubles, and desires as you weave her story threads through your novel.

TIMELINES

The second technique I used while writing *A Certain Slant of Light* was a timeline, a list of events in the plot written from left to right along a horizontal line in chronological order, often broken into logical sections. Similar to the plot web, the timeline helped me keep the story and characters in order, from major plot points to small details. Using the timeline, I could decide if my bits of action were smartly ordered, see where I might need to insert setups and payoffs, and shape my story correctly, building to the climax, the overarching crosshairs of my book. A timeline can also help prevent you from embarrassing mistakes like having your characters' kids going to school on a Saturday or having two full moons ten days apart.

A timeline can be broken into acts, but for *A Certain Slant of Light*, I used three blocks of time: "Helen Light/ James in body" (this covers everything that happens from the beginning of the story—where Helen, the protagonist, is an intangible spirit and James is a ghost using the body of a teenaged boy—until a body is located for Helen to possess), "Both in bodies" (from the time Helen enters the body of a teenaged girl to the moment she realizes James has left a physical body), and "Helen in body/James gone" (from the moment Helen thinks she has been left behind to the end of the book). I planted various events in order along this line within these three sections because it helped me remember how far I needed to progress in various subplots before major turning points (like entering and exiting bodies) took place. Using a timeline kept me from sitting and staring at the computer screen trying to review the order of events in my head. And, as with the plot web, I avoided having to rework a passage to fill in a missed setup or subplot.

To get an overview of what a timeline might entail, here are timelines for two well-known stories as examples:

Little Red Riding Hood

At Red's House

- Red is given a basket of goodies
- Red is instructed to go to Grandma's
- Red is warned not to talk to anyone on the way

In Woods

- Red meets Wolf, and he likes the smell of the goodies
- Wolf lies to Red about a good shortcut
- Red believes Wolf and takes the shortcut that is really a longcut
- Wolf takes the true shortcut to Grandma's

At Grandma's

- Wolf gets to the house first and eats Grandma
- Wolf dresses like Grandma and gets in her bed
- Wolf greets Red as Grandma when Red arrives
- Red points out three unusual things about Grandma
- Wolf makes up reasons not to worry about those clues
- Wolf is revealed and chases Red around

- Woodsman shows up and fells Wolf, cutting him open and dumping out Grandma

- Red and Grandma are reunited

A Christmas Carol

In Past

- We hear that Marley died on Christmas Eve seven years before the story starts

Things That Happen Before Marley Visits

- Cratchit gets on Scrooge's nerves

- Caroling boys are chased off

- Gentlemen asking for donations are rejected

- Nephew's invitation is rejected

- Scrooge thinks he sees apparitions, but he does not believe them

During Marley's Visit

- Marley introduces Scrooge to the concept of the hauntings

During Christmas Past

- Scrooge sees his childhood and sister

- Scrooge sees his old boss and his long lost sweetheart

During Christmas Present

- Scrooge sees the Cratchits
- Scrooge sees his nephew

During Christmas Yet to Come

- Scrooge sees that the Cratchits have lost Tiny Tim
- Scrooge sees that there is rejoicing at the death of an unknown man
- Scrooge discovers that he is the dead man

After Waking

- Scrooge celebrates
- Scrooge passes out presents
- Scrooge gives Cratchit a raise and promises to help

In the Future

- We hear that Scrooge followed through and was a good man ever after

You might want to section off your story by location, if that makes sense. *The Wizard of Oz* would work well that way: things that happen in Kansas, in the Munchkin City, on the Yellow Brick Road, in the Emerald City, on the way to the witch's castle, at the castle, back in the Emerald City, and back in Kansas.

But if you were writing a novel with one location, like a haunted house story that takes place almost entirely in one building, you could break up the plot according to what the characters think or believe: things that happened before anything odd has been experienced, strange things happen but are not believed to be supernatural, a haunting is obvious but the characters don't know who the ghost is, they think they know who the ghost is but are mistaken, they realize who's really haunting the house, they bring in help and clear the house, and things that happen after the clearing.

You'll know what best fits your own story. And again, this may not be your kind of technique. If you can write well and quickly with a traditional outline, or with nothing at all, write away.

PLOT MENU

Another technique that might help those who prefer not to use typical outlines is the plot menu. You list things that will need to happen at some point (usually in the order that they should occur) in categories and cross them out as you take care of them. You can use this technique anytime, from the beginning stages of idea generation to the reworking of the book, and you can use it with or without an outline. It's simply another visual aid to remind you of all the storylines, subplots, and minor characters. If you create a plot menu before you start your novel, you could write general concepts and refine them as you compose. If you're halfway through a draft, you could list the plot points you've already covered first and continue the list into things that haven't yet happened. The plot menu would then be a tool to help you track what still needs to be covered in the story.

Here is *Romeo and Juliet* by William Shakespeare categorized by character:

- **Romeo:** has a crush on another girl, falls in love with Juliet at first sight, woos her and secretly weds her, does not want to feud with J's family anymore, tries to keep Tybalt and Mercutio from fighting, kills Tybalt, is banished, believes J is dead, kills himself

- **Juliet:** falls in love with Romeo at a ball, sends nurse to Romeo with message, marries R in secret, loves him even when she finds out he has killed her cousin, balks at marrying Paris, gets a drug from the Friar and appears dead, wakes to find Romeo dead, kills herself

- **Mercutio:** teases Romeo, begins a fight with Tybalt that is mostly playful, is killed and curses the feuding families with his last breath

- **Friar:** warns Romeo about having a hasty heart, weds R & J despite foreboding, helps Romeo escape when banished, gives J potion and explains plan, tries to help R & J run away together, flees when plan fails

- **Nurse:** helps Juliet wed Romeo, advises her to forget her new husband and marry Paris

- **Juliet's father:** makes a marriage contract with Paris, rages at daughter for refusing Paris, mourns daughter's apparent death

- **Juliet's mother:** gives Juliet advice in hopes of preparing her for marriage, is appalled by her refusal of Paris, mourns her daughter's apparent death

- **Prince:** stops a street fight between feuding Montagues and Capulets, banishes Romeo, makes morality speech at end

A plot menu doesn't have to list actions only. A romance, for instance, could be filled with emotions that change, grow, and fade.

Fictional Love Story Plot Menu

- **Joe:** starts out indifferent to Mary, becomes attracted to her, falls in love with her, is disillusioned about her (mistaken), falls back in love with her, finds out the truth of her innocence

- **Mary:** starts out hating Joe, is annoyed by becoming attracted to him and hides her feelings, is startled to discover he's not as bad as she thought, falls in love with him, is confused by his coldness, finds out by the end that her feelings are returned

- **Stella:** starts out attracted to but not in love with Joe, is jealous of his attention to Mary and tries to win his affections, is frustrated and tries to talk Mary out of liking him, is further frustrated and gives up

- **Bruce:** starts out interested in Mary and is tolerant of her indifference to him, finds himself attracted to

Stella against his better judgment, turns his attentions on Stella, is disturbed by her obsession with Joe and Mary, turns away from Stella and moves on

Plot webs, timelines, and plot menus may or may not work for you—the important thing is to prepare yourself for writing quickly and well. What you want to avoid is unnecessary restarts and tossed pages—do whatever you need to do to clear the decks when you prepare to take off writing.

CHAPTER 7

STEALING TRICKS FROM THE BEST

If you read good books, when you write,
good books will come out of you.

—Natalie Goldberg

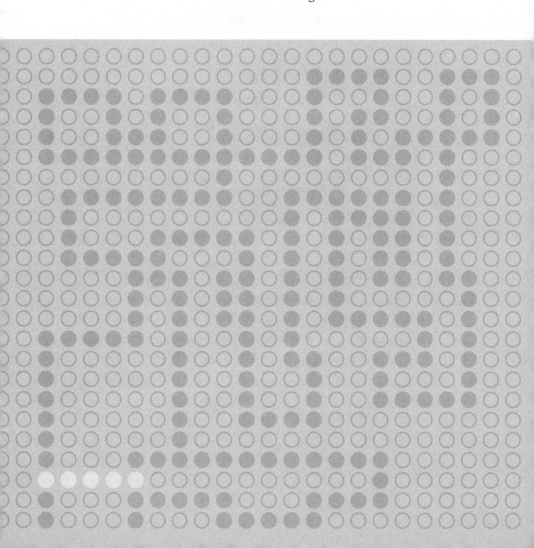

It isn't exactly tricks that we're going to steal, but wisdom. And it's not really stealing because we're not lifting material from other writers. We're simply learning by example how to make our own novels better.

When you're trying to write a great draft quickly, you don't want to keep rewriting a tricky scene over and over, and you don't want to sit there staring at the blank page, unsure where to begin. Instead, reread scenes from some of your favorite novels and take note of the techniques and structures that worked so well for them. Here are examples of situations in which best-selling writers taught me by example.

THE EMOTIONAL CRACK

When a character is changed forever by some rupture in his world, when his heart is broken, his spirit crushed, his brave façade ripped away, the readers gain insight into his humanity. This is an emotional crack scene. Antagonists can crack, just as protagonists do. These are crucial scenes because they give important depth to a main character and because they are usually tied to a major turning point in the second or third act of a story. A hero is tested, a villain is made more three-dimensional, a character shows his vulnerability so that his intended can fall in love with him. There are many places within a story where an emotional crack can make your novel better. If you need a character to crumble or have an emotional upheaval that she overcomes, but you are having trouble with the scene, think about these four guidelines:

1. Throw something at your character that is the opposite of what she is used to dealing with.

2. Take your time.

3. Use the details around the character to mirror the emotions of the scene.

4. Use other characters to contrast with the person who is cracking.

In Charles Dickens's *Nicholas Nickleby*, the villain, Nicholas's uncle Ralph, is made unexpectedly vulnerable when he recalls his former capacity to love and be loved.

> As the door of the vehicle was roughly closed, a comb fell from Kate's hair, close to her uncle's feet; and as he picked it up, and returned it into her hand, the light from a neighbouring lamp shone upon her face. The lock of hair that had escaped and curled loosely over her brow, the traces of tears yet scarcely dry, the flushed cheek, the look of sorrow, all fired some dormant train of recollection in the old man's breast; and the face of his dead brother seemed present before him, with the very look it bore on some occasion of boyish grief, of which every minutest circumstance flashed upon his mind, with the distinctness of a scene of yesterday.

Ralph Nickleby, who was proof against all appeals of blood and kindred—who was steeled against every tale of sorrow and distress—staggered while he looked, and went back into his house, as a man who had seen a spirit from some world beyond the grave.

Notice how Dickens crafted this scene.

1. **He gave Ralph something uncharacteristic to do.** Ralph helps his niece into her carriage, a gesture of etiquette with which he would not normally bother.

2. **Dickens took his time.** He used more than 150 words to describe a moment that would have lasted perhaps ten seconds in real life.

3. **Dickens used details to mirror emotions.** The lighting has an otherworldly nostalgia; the carriage implies a certain urgency; the comb is a lost object, something he never would have noticed except that it is fallen. It's like a piece of a memory jarred free.

4. **Dickens used the character of Kate in contrast with her uncle and what he is experiencing.** Ralph is unused to expressing his feelings, and Kate freely weeps. He is out of touch with his childhood self, and she is the picture of innocence and youth.

When I was writing *Judas Cross*, the biblical novel that would later win me a modest fellowship, I needed to create a scene in which my antihero was stricken with a painful memory. I knew it would be that excerpt from Dickens I would use as inspiration:

> Here the boy's head lowered and rested on his neck, taking nest in the cold hollow of his collarbone. One strand of hair blew against his throat, the tickle stirring some dormant sorrow. Every sensation of the only embrace he had ever shared with Brother rose up wild and hot in his chest: a strand of Brother's hair blowing against his forehead, their sandals touching, the gold flash of lamplight in Brother's dark eyes as he turned to kiss him. The memory lashed at him from under his ribs and then curled back, contorting his dead heart into ice.

I didn't copy the plot line. In the Dickens excerpt, we see the antagonist, having just caused his niece great shame, recall a moment from his childhood. In my excerpt, we see the protagonist, while sitting in an alley beside a dying boy, recall his last evening with his dearest friend.

And I didn't copy the syntax or semantics. There were only five words of any significance used in both passages: curled, sorrow, hair, dormant, and dead.

What I did take from the two Dickens paragraphs was the emotion. I paid attention to the way the author slowed everything down and how he let the readers feel the significance of each image rather than explaining, for example, why a flushed cheek was heartbreaking.

I tried to do what Dickens had done.

1. **I gave my protagonist an uncharacteristic activity.** He's a loner who walks the earth ignoring humans, so I made him responsible for saving a human to whom he has suddenly and inexplicably become attached.

2. **I took my time.** I carefully stretched the flash of recognition into a hundred words.

3. **I used details to mirror the emotions.** He's feeling haunted, so the boy's hair tickles him like a spectral hand getting his attention. And the memory doesn't just come into his mind; it rises in his chest like a ghost.

4. **I made the other character my protagonist's opposite.** My main character (a vampire) wants to die but cannot, so the boy he's befriended is dying.

Whether your emotional crack scene has dialogue or is nonverbal, whether it takes place in the middle of the manuscript or at the dramatic climax, these guidelines should help the scene work better.

THE SEX SCENE

For some people, writing sex scenes is a tricky business. How many should there be? Where do they go? How much should

I show? There aren't easy answers for these questions. Some novels have no sex scenes; some have many. They can happen early on or not until near the end of the book. Some sex scenes show almost nothing; others are quite explicit. Here are three guidelines that may help:

1. **The sex scene should add to the story.** Just like any scene, it has to have a purpose. To simply arouse or entertain is not a good enough reason to write a sex scene. If you could cut it and the story would be unchanged, it doesn't belong in the novel. It needs to move the story along.

2. **The sex scene should be true to the characters.** It's fine to have your characters behaving differently than they normally would—that's common when people give way to passion—but they need to be consistent. If the readers have latched onto these people and they act out of character in the sex scene, it will feel fake and be less effective. To be true to your story, make sure your sex scene includes character development. Your lovers are changed in some way by the scene. What has shifted?

3. **The sex scene should fit the style of your novel.** Just as comic romps are written differently than science fiction thrillers, your sex scene needs to match your genre and your writing style. If, when your characters make love, it feels like you switched from a gritty detective thriller to a historical romance, your readers will be confused and annoyed.

Also, here are some tips to avoid sounding cliché:

1. **Don't use textbook names for body parts.** This takes readers out of the moment. Honestly, you don't even have to refer to body parts. We all know which gadgets are used in the sex act.

2. **Don't use goofy names for body parts.** Unless you're writing a farce.

3. **Don't have the lovers in your novel talk like porn stars.** Thanks to Steve Almond for teaching this in his delightful article, "Writing Sex" (*The Boston Phoenix*, April 25, 2003). Okay, I don't have a lot of experience with this and Almond's article is charming, so just go find it on the Web and read it.

4. **Don't let the rhythm of the act create a plateau.** I've only seen snippets of a few X-rated movies, but they bored me. You could take the actress off the actor and put a different gal in her place and the actor seems like he wouldn't care or even notice. A sex scene in a novel is like any other scene: It has a goal, creates tension, and includes character development. If you have your lovers bounce along in the sex act too long without these three scene elements, the sex will become flat and boring.

5. **Don't write overly exaggerated climaxes.** If the orgasm is too corny, the reader will start criticizing your writing instead of enjoying the scene.

6. **At the risk of sounding sexist, don't have your male character describe your female character's clothes.** (Unless, again, you're writing a comedy.) A man will probably be aware that a woman's clothes are revealing or a certain color, but he isn't likely to know the fabrics or the specific names for the bustier, corset, or camisole.

In an early scene from *Prodigal Summer*, Barbara Kingsolver has two of her characters, Deanna and Eddie, make love for the first time on the porch of Deanna's cabin in the woods. What made it so erotic wasn't just that the lovers were so excited that they didn't make it into the house before they had sex or that they barely knew each other. There was something else about it that I couldn't explain at first. But when I was about to write the scene in which my ghosts first make love in *A Certain Slant of Light*, I went back to *Prodigal Summer* and looked more closely at what Kingsolver was doing.

> She bent down to him, tasting the salt skin of his chest with the sensitive tip of her tongue, and then exploring the tight drum of his abdomen. He shuddered at the touch of her breath on his skin, giving her to know that she could take and own Eddie Bondo. It was the body's decision, a body with no more choice of its natural history than an orchid has, or the bee it needs, and so they would both get lost here, she would let him

in, anywhere he wanted to go. In the last full hour of daylight, while lacewings sought solace for their brief lives in the forest's bright upper air, and the husk of her empty nylon parka lay tangled with his in the mud, their two soft-skinned bodies completed their introductions on the floor of her porch. A breeze shook rain out of new leaves onto their hair, but in their pursuit of eternity they never noticed the chill.

Certainly the scene added to the story and moved the action along. It was character appropriate. It fit the style of the novel perfectly. It was far from cliché, but there was something else at work, I could tell. It wasn't just that she used atypical details (no more choice than an orchid; an empty parka) or that she held back some of them (it isn't until later, when Deanna is daydreaming about him, that the readers get a description of Eddie's facial expression); it was also that Kingsolver turned our gaze away from the sex act. She began with the lovers, then she pulled back and away, up into the trees to see and hear and feel the nature surrounding them. But the lovers didn't pause; the sex continued in the readers' minds.

I tried Kingsolver's technique for my own characters, Helen and James, in the lovers' bed they made in the loft of an empty high school theater:

All around us the shadows pulsed with the rhythm of his sounds, a whisper breath with each thrust. My answers as soft as bird talk.

The invisible depths above shifted with hidden ropes and dark lights like the hushed sway of limbs in night trees.

When you compose your sex scene, look up sex scenes in your favorite novels and see if you can learn other tricks from the authors you admire.

Recommended Reading

Here are some books about great books—you never know where you might find inspiration.

- *Great Books* by David Denby: This book tends to list classics.

- *Book Sense Best Books: 125 Favorite Books Recommended by Independent Booksellers*: This book focuses on more recent works.

- *1,001 Books You Must Read Before You Die* by Peter Ackroyd and Peter Boxall

- *Books that Changed the World* by Robert B. Downs

THE AWE-INSPIRING ENTRANCE

When I was in ninth grade, I heard Ray Bradbury tell the now-legendary story of how Herman Melville was composing a dry and dispassionate book on whaling until he was introduced to the works of Shakespeare, after which he turned his project into *Moby-Dick*. Melville, overcome with a sudden understanding of what makes storytelling magnificent, wrote the opening sentence ("Call me Ishmael."), and he was never the same.

When you are about to introduce your readers to a new character, look back at a description from one of your favorite authors and see what they did that burned that image into your mind.

In her novel *The Heaven Tree*, Edith Pargeter describes the appearance and "landing" of an angel. Had she been Melville before the Shakespearean rapture, or just one of us, she might have written this:

> The angel landed gracefully, his arms open to the light above. He had a youthful face and long, golden hair. He averted his sparkling eyes from the brightness, and his powerful body was poised and waiting.

But here are the actual opening lines from Pargeter's *The Heaven Tree*:

> The angel, eternally alighting with arched wings and delicate, stretched feet, spread his hands palms outwards towards the radiance, and bowed in ceremonious humility

the youthful, narrow head, with long gold hair still erect and quivering from his flight. The shuddering hum of his great wings hung perpetually upon the astonished air, for ever stilling and never stilled. His eyes, half-averted from the unbearable brightness, had themselves a brilliance not to be borne, and his face was as taut and fierce as the body arrested for ever in the instant of alighting, straining downwards from breast to loin to thigh to instep, silver sinews braced and quivering under the frozen turmoil of the gilded robe. He touched the earth with long, naked, shapely feet, and the earth gave forth a brazen cry, and the tremulous air vibrated like a bowstring along the descending arc of his passage from heaven.

In the shadowy spaces above him the creator bent his head to look upon his work, and saw that it was good.

Here are some things to keep in mind when you introduce a character for the first time:

1. **Sound a call to attention.** The way you word the entrance should be a clue to the readers that something new is happening. You could use the narrator, in an old-fashioned storytelling style, to present the character, like on the first page of *The Phantom Tollbooth* by Norton Juster: "There was once a boy

named Milo who didn't know what to do with himself ..." You could do as Christopher Moore did in *Lamb* and have one character announce the new character in dialogue: "'Arise, Levi who is called Biff.'" Or you could do as Chuck Palahniuk does in *Fight Club* and make a statement: "This is how I met Marla Singer." Do whatever fits your style, but try to use wording that tells your readers they should pay attention.

2. **Make your character stand out.** If your character is striking to the eye, like the angel in the example from *The Heaven Tree*, she will certainly catch the readers' attention. But if the character you are introducing is not physically different from the other characters, or if he blends into the environment visually, make sure the character behaves in a way that captures the readers' interest. In *Gone With the Wind* by Margaret Mitchell, there may have been lots of interesting men at the Wilkes's party, but only one that gave Scarlett an "embarrassed sensation that her dress was too low in the bosom." Rhett instantly stands out for the reader because he stands out for the protagonist.

3. **Don't bury your character's entrance.** If you introduce a new character in the middle of a description of something else (like another character, the setting, or a summary of action), the introduction will be less powerful and your readers might

even miss it completely. Start a fresh paragraph when you bring in your new character. Give him the spotlight and center stage as Pargeter did with her angel. In *Oldest Living Confederate Widow Tells All* by Allan Gurganus, when the protagonist introduces her husband, she doesn't hide it in a paragraph about herself, her situation, her feelings, or her age. She begins the story with these words: "Died on me finally. He had to. Died doing his bad bugle imitation, calling for the maps, died bellowing orders at everybody, horses included ..." Gurganus made sure the Colonel's entrance was the beginning of a paragraph and that the character description was memorable.

4. **Use dialogue to lift your character out of the crowd.** Not all entrances include dialogue—the Pargeter example, for instance, does not—but if the character you are introducing speaks when he first appears, make sure he speaks differently from anyone else or have what he says raise him above the crowd. In *Soldier in the Rain* by William Goldman, the character of Maxwell Slaughter is made distinct and beloved by his first line of dialogue. It's not that he uses words differently. He stands out because he doesn't say what we expect him to. Eustis Clay, a strangely childish fellow, crawls into Max's office performing an impromptu death scene. "'Tell ... Colonel ... Custer,' he whispered, his face contorted with pain. 'Tell ... him ... the ...

Little Big Horn ... is ... a ... tr—' He fell over backward and lay still." The reader might expect Max to respond by saying something like, "You're an idiot," or, "Get up, you damn fool," but instead he applauds: "'Moving,' he said. 'Undeniably moving.'" From that moment I understood what kind of book I was reading. And I knew from Max's first line that I would love him.

So look at your character introductions. Do you call the readers to attention? Is the character distinctive? Do you bring her in at the opening of a paragraph? If she speaks, does what she says capture the readers' interest?

Fun Stuff

- Try interviewing trusted friends who have good taste about what I call the "I wish I'd thought of that" moments in their favorite novels, plays, movies, or TV shows. Get a small notebook and every time you have a few extra minutes with a writer support group friend or colleague (waiting for a bus, before the food arrives at a restaurant, while sunbathing at the beach) interview her, making note of the interviewee's name, the work she is referring to, its author, the passage she is remarking on, and why the passage was a coveted one. Look up these passages and decide whether you agree. See what you can learn from the glowing moments described.

- Go back to the picture books that were your favorites in childhood. Read one out loud. It may bring back echoes of early inspiration.

MIXED PERCEPTION

A mixed perception scene, one in which the author creates tension or enhances character development by making sure the action can be interpreted in at least two ways, is tricky to pull off but effective when you get it right. When I wanted to write a scene in which the action was perceived in a certain way by one character and quite differently by another, I recalled a scene from *White Butterfly* by Walter Mosley in which the narrator, Easy Rawlins, comes home drunk and has sex with his wife.

> Regina let me hold her. She buried her face against my neck while I worked off my shorts and shirt. But when I moved to enter her she turned away from me. All of this was new. Regina wasn't as wild about sex as I was but she would usually come close to matching

my ardor. Now it was like she wanted me but with nothing coming from her.

It excited me all the more, and even though I was dizzy with the alcohol in my blood, I cozied up behind her and entered her the way dogs do it.

"Stop, Easy!" she cried, but I knew she meant, "Go on, do it!"

She writhed and I clamped my legs around hers. I bucked up against her and she grabbed the night table with such force that it was knocked over on to the floor. The lamp was pulled from the electric plug and the room went dark.

"Oh, God no!" she cried and she came, shouting and bucking and elbowing me hard.

When I relaxed my hold she pushed away and got up. I remember the light coming on and her standing there in the harsh electric glare. There was sweat on her face and glistening in her pubic hair. She looked at me with an emotion I could not read.

"I love you," I said.

I passed into sleep before her answer.

From his perspective it was passion. But the next morning, as we hear Regina telling her side, we realize it was something else.

"You don't hit me but you do other things just as bad."

"Like what?"

Regina was looking at my hands. I looked down myself to see clenched fists.

"Last night," she said. "What you call that?"

"Call what?"

"What you did to me. I didn't want none'a you. But you made me. You raped me."

"Rape?" I laughed. "Man caint rape his own wife."

Mosley chooses his words carefully as he describes the attack. Because the scene was from a first-person narrated novel, some phrases were true only from his perspective: *she wanted me, I cozied up behind her, I knew she meant, "Go on, do it!", she came.* Some phrases are ones she might have included in her own telling of the story: *she turned away from me, I was dizzy with alcohol, "Stop, Easy!", she grabbed the night table with such force it was knocked over, "Oh, God no!", elbowing me hard.* And some phrases were somewhere in between: *Regina let me hold her* and *she writhed.* The end result is effective because, as we are reading the scene the first time, we believe Easy's take on the situation, although we feel something isn't quite right. Afterward we are disturbed because we see the same scene from Regina's point of view. We actually feel guilty because we didn't realize it sooner. Talk about tension. And the scene adds to character development because we can see how Easy's troubles and drinking are destroying his integrity and his marriage.

Here is how I used that technique to make the following scene from *Judas Cross* seem like an impersonal feeding to the vampire antihero and like a rape to the female victim:

> He had come upon a green-eyed woman washing clothes on a rock at the edge of the Nile somewhere in his second century of wandering. It was unusual, and to the woman's misfortune, that she was alone. He caught her from behind, surprised that one so slim could put up as good a struggle as most men. He had her arms pinned to her and drove her to her knees. She tried to kick him, but he was pressed to her back. He pushed down until she was kneeling and he was laying over her like a heavy animal skin. He held both her arms with one of his own now, and with his other hand he forced his fingers into her black hair and twisted her head to one side. His teeth slid in easily and her blood was glorious—liquid heat and honey melon. She worked all the while he drank from her, straining to claw at his arm, trying to squirm out from under him, her knees digging into the soil.

Having studied Mosley's example, I tried to choose my words carefully. As for the attacker, the vampire comments unemotionally on the fact that she is alone and therefore easy to attack; he describes subduing her the way someone might describe a calf being roped and tied. He notices she is strong for her size, but shows no interest in her body, only in her blood. As for the victim, I hope I gave the readers a sense of what she is experiencing so they can empathize with her. I want them to feel like the victim, like the food that is being devoured:She tries to kick him; she fights with such determination he has to lay his full weight over her before she is driven to her knees; even after being pinned down she continues to fight even if all she can manage to do is to scratch his arms. Hopefully in this way the readers experience both sides of the event. In this case the mixed perception scene adds tension because the readers are in the skin of the antihero and yet sympathize with the victim. And it adds to character development because it gives the readers a deeper understanding of how detached from human suffering the antihero has become.

If you want to write a mixed perception scene, try these three steps:

1. Make a note of how the scene you are planning will increase the tension in the story.

2. Make a list of what the scene will tell the readers about the characters involved. Will secrets be revealed? Will the readers understand something new about a character's wounds? Will the scene show us what makes a character tick?

3. Now write two paragraphs, one from each side of the situation, in the words of the characters in the scene who have different takes on the action. The cop and the person being arrested, the teacher and the student, the dogcatcher and the dog. Look at the two descriptions and see if there are words or phrases that might be borrowed from each paragraph and intermingled to form one scene with dual perspectives.

So far I have talked about special kinds of scenes that you can learn about from other writers. But there are special moments that can be tricky to write, as well: moment of foreshadowing and a moment that sends a chill through your readers.

FORESHADOWING

In Steven Sherrill's *Visits from the Drowned Girl*, the rough and informal narrator becomes suddenly poetic, in his gritty way, when describing the dry streambed behind an old fish merchant's house:

> Tick Freeze was the reigning Filet King; when his knife was sharp, and it was always sharp, Tick could skin and gut a catfish in thirty seconds. Put the filets, wrapped in newspaper, in your hand in forty-five.
>
> But what do you do with the ropy wet guts and comblike spines and the barbed heads—with their dimming fish eyes—of all

those catfish? The Freezes, generations of Freezes, gathered the innards in tin buckets, a day's worth at a time, and flung them, a red shower of viscera, into the gully behind their house. Catfish bark when you pull them out of the water. Guttural little yips of protest. Some say that if you walked past the gully behind Freeze's house at night, you'd hear the ghosts of the dead catfish, years and years of dead catfish swimming the dry banks, that you'd hear the guts and spines still barking. Crying out. That if you walk up to the edge of the gully, at night, you'd see all those catfish eyes looking up at you glinting in the milky moonlight.

It's startling because it's unexpected, unlike the antihero's previous voice, but more important, it's gripping because it foreshadows his relationship with death, something we don't fully grasp until the end of the book. When I want to write a foreshadowing moment, I often think of those barking fish spines.

If you think your manuscript needs a moment like this, when something significant in the a major character's future is foreshadowed, see if any of these hints help:

1. Something in the setting or in the character's surroundings might make a minor shift similar to the major one that's coming. A villain soon to be caught finds his pet dog tangled in his leash, trapped.

2. Something could happen to a minor character that will mirror the future of your main character. In the penultimate chapter, your protagonist's maid says she must give notice because she is getting married, foreshadowing that your hero will find true love by the last chapter.

3. A subplot may foreshadow the outcome of a major plot point. An argument lost at home can foreshadow a case lost in the courtroom if your hero is a lawyer.

4. Foreshadowing could come in the way your character perceives something, giving a hint at a shift in emotions, such as the fish spine example. A character who will rise to heroic heights describes something he was previously frightened of as if it is no longer a threat. A character who will open her heart sees the love in her parents' relationship for the first time.

CHILLING MOMENTS

Perhaps you want to create a moment that will make your readers shiver with horror. How do horror and suspense writers frighten us with so few words? It's all about setting the stage. If you can front-load the readers with the right details, the readers' imagination fills in the blanks later with powerful imagery made all the more terrifying because it has been personalized.

In *The Exorcist* by William Peter Blatty, readers have been given the following pieces of information:

1. There is something very wrong with Chris's little girl, Regan. She is being heavily sedated after unexplained episodes of bizarre behavior during which she often demonstrated grotesque feats of strength.

2. A friend of Chris's came to the apartment and stayed for a while when Chris and the babysitter were out of the flat. He was gone by the time they returned and was later found dead at the foot of the outdoor steps below the child's bedroom window.

3. During the police interview with Chris, the detective, Kinderman, explains that the man's neck had been broken by having his head turned completely backward; therefore, the murderer must have been a powerful man.

4. The detective asks if the dead man could have fallen from Regan's window, but Chris tells him the shutters are always kept closed.

5. The detective asks if Regan might have witnessed a struggle with an intruder, but Chris says the child was unconscious, heavily drugged.

6. The detective asks if he might speak to the girl anyway, but Chris says she is asleep.

With these concepts implanted in our minds, Blatty describes what the detective sees from his car as he's about to drive off.

> When he'd entered the passenger side of the squad car, Kinderman turned and looked back at the house. He thought he saw movement at Regan's window, a quick, lithe figure flashing to the side and out of view. He wasn't sure. He'd seen it peripherally as he'd turned. But he noted that the shutters were open. Odd. For a moment he waited. No one appeared.

The author only needed to use sixty-five words. The readers are the ones who imagine who is at that window. The readers are the ones who see a small figure climb from the bed, despite the drugs that promised to keep her asleep. The readers are the ones who are haunted by the possible expressions distorting the face of the lithe creature who hides beside that window casement. It's the readers who keep replaying this short scene long after they have closed the book and turned out the bedside lamp.

When you plan your chilling moment, use this this checklist as a guide:

1. Do the readers have all the background information they need to understand what's creepy about the moment? In the example from *The Exorcist*, the moment would have been much less disturbing if we didn't know the girl was heavily drugged.

2. Are the readers grounded in reality to make the moment terrifying in contrast? If everything around you is already dark and eerie, a bump in the night is not particularly spooky. Remind the readers what normal life is like, what is natural and sweet about reality, so that the horror will be darker by contrast. If Regan had been a foul-mouthed, drug-abusing teen before she was possessed by the devil, Blatty would have offset the terror. Instead he made sure Regan was as cute and innocent as can be so that when her breath begins to smell like death and a deep voice comes from her throat, it is shocking by comparison.

3. Are you giving the readers enough room to drive themselves crazy? Leave something to the imagination. Make the readers do most of the work. Tell just enough, not too much. If Blatty had made the child easily visible in the window frame and had described exactly what she looked like, it might have been creepy, but it would have been all there on the page. The unknown is always scarier because we can't help thinking, *was it too horrible to even describe?*

LISTENING TO YOUR GHOSTS

If you're like me, sometimes while you are writing, something shows up in your mind that you can't explain. Why did you think of that nursery rhyme while you were trying to write that scene at the military school? Why did you keep singing that hymn when you were trying to write the conversation between the doctor and his doorman? Honor those ghosts of ideas that come to haunt you. They came to visit for a reason. Something in your subconscious is telling you to look to that piece of poetry or line of song lyrics for inspiration. It's the same as looking at novels to learn how to write tricky scenes, only in this case the inspiration comes to you. You are meant to take the emotions, rhythm, language, or mood (or all of the above) of that song or poem and use it to improve your novel.

Borrowing the Rhythm and Emotion

When I was on the brink of writing a critical passage in my first novel, I hesitated because I didn't know how to communicate the right tone. Helen, my dead protagonist, was recalling the last moments of her life when she hoped to save her little girl whom she believes died in the same accident that killed her. The scene needed to express a combination of hope and regret. I let my mind wander and was visited by the memory of another moment that held for me that particular mix of emotions.

What came to mind was a song by Leslie Bricusse from the musical *Scrooge* in which the old man remembers the girl he loved and lost in his youth. Those lyrics probably came to haunt me because in both these cases, the scene foreshadows a kind of salvation—Scrooge will get a second chance to be a good man; Helen will soon discover her baby did survive after all.

Bricusse's song "You ... You" ended with a rhythmic, five-pulse longing.

> You, my only hope.
> You, my only love.
> You. You. You.

I structured Helen's thoughts in a similar rhythm, not so much because readers would need those five beats to feel the ghost's pain, but because using the rhythm of the Bricusse song resonated the emotion within *me*, and that helped me choose the right words.

From *A Certain Slant of Light*:

> You, my only child. You, my only friend. Don't
> wait. Run. *Live.*

Borrowing the Language and Mood

When I was creating a psalm set for the Fetches (death escorts) in my novel, *The Fetch*, I wanted the poetry to be original yet sound familiar to readers. A series of poems came into my mind and I listed them. They were like spirits coming to assist me, and I tinted each psalm with a little of each lyric's language and mood. I think this gave the psalms a certain historical resonance. This technique, borrowing from lyrics, gave the verses an undertone of realism as if (at least subconsciously) Fetch psalms sound like ancient documents from which the *earthly* poems were later derived.

As an inspiration and form, for Fetch Psalm Three I studied stanza 7 from John Keats's "Ode to a Nightingale":

Thou wast not born for death, immortal
    Bird!
No hungry generations tread thee down;
The voice I hear this passing night was
    heard
In ancient days by emperor and clown:
Perhaps the self-same song that found a
    path
Through the sad heart of Ruth, when, sick
    for home,
She stood in tears amid the alien corn;
The same that oft-times hath
Charm'd magic casements, opening on the
    foam
Of perilous seas, in faery lands forlorn.

I borrowed the number of lines and line lengths, the style of language, and the general tone of the Keats poem without actually borrowing the content or any important words.

Fetch Psalm Three, "Call for the Dead":

Fear not, for you will never be alone;
Each child of woman walks the earth a
    while
And whether over cloverleaf or stone,
Step by step, draws closer to the Aisle.
Now slip from shell and take the offered
    hand;
In disguise the holy gift is given.
Dust of His dust, stranger to this land,

Wake and hear the music of His heav'n.

Come and join the inescapable march.

Pass beneath the opalescent arch.

Once I even took the philosophy of a song in a rock opera to inspire one of my novel's crosshairs scenes. Don't fight your ghosts. Take inspiration when it materializes.

As you write your first draft, take time to look back at works of genius that have inspired you. Notice how your literary heroes cleared the types of stumbling blocks you are facing. It will save rewriting later if you let others guide you to your own greatness.

CHAPTER 8

FAST TRACK TO THE DEEPER EMOTION

No tears in the writer, no tears in the reader.
—Robert Frost

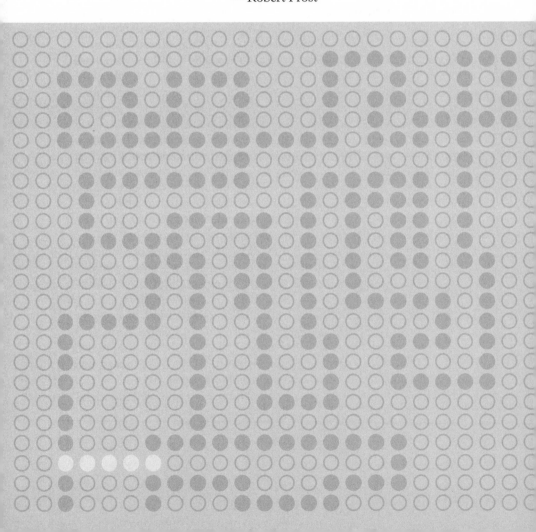

The novels we remember all our lives are the ones that move us. And now you are the novelist; you are the one given the chance to touch the readers emotionally. If you can make the readers angry when your hero is betrayed, give them chills when your villain gets the upper hand, make them laugh at your characters' bumblings, or weep when your characters are grieving, you and your novel will be loved and remembered.

If you don't tap into the deep emotion in your story, if you skim over the scenes where your characters' feelings are revealed, your story will read as shallow, hollow, forgettable. You could always go back and retrace your steps with a lot of rewriting, but wouldn't it be better to get at that emotion in your first draft?

For me the inspiration I get from art and especially music is immeasurable. They are my shortcuts into the emotion of my story. When the pictures posted around me and the music playing in my office take me into the mood of the story, I can write that story with greater speed and with deeper emotion. It's almost like being able to make myself have a certain dream when I go to sleep at night. I create an environment that brings my story into my mind and heart when I sit down to write every day.

Your story may involve many different emotions, but every story has a central mood. One story might be about regret, another about romantic longing, another about heroic adventure. When I start writing a new project, I make sure that I have the music and the pictures that match the mood of my story.

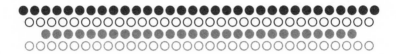

Recommended Viewing

- *Art: A World History* by Elke Linda Buch-holz, Susanne Kaeppele, Karoline Hille, and Irina Stotland

- *Seizing the Light: A History of Photography* by Robert Hirsch

USING ART

They say a picture paints a thousand words. When I was a kid, I assumed this meant that it would take a thousand words to describe everything there was to see in a single picture. But as a writer I know it means that visual art communicates volumes. You can help inspire yourself with the right art in your workspace. Art not only gives you an instant shot of beauty, it brings up emotions, poses questions, acts as a sort of muse.

> • **Setting.** Find visuals that represent your setting, either literally (a photograph of the very same World War II restaurant where your hero and villain meet) or symbolically (a painting of a French village

celebration that holds the essence of your German garden wedding).

- **Characters.** In the same way, you can find pictures— photographs of people or statues, drawings, prints of paintings—that either look like your characters (or are your characters, if you write about real people) or represent a character. A photo of a fifteen-year-old boy from the 1930s may hold in his eyes the essence of your contemporary thirty-year-old hero. The only thing that matters is that you get a charge out of the art. It makes you feel inspired and engaged. You might even put up pictures of the people you want to star in the movie version of your novel. Don't judge it. Just do whatever works for you.

- **Details.** Sometimes I have strange pictures up on my board that don't look like places or people: a certain kind of axe handle, the leaves of a particular plant. These are research details that I needed in order to write a scene, but I liked them visually enough to keep them on display.

Remember to be open-minded in your search for images. You may find pictures in magazines, postcards from friends who traveled through Europe, pages torn from museum catalogs, old family photos that appeal to you and connect with your novel in ways you can't explain. That's okay. That's more than okay. That's wonderful. Because the more a piece of art strikes straight at the heart without touching the brain, the better. That's where you need to be touched by the art in order to be inspired and revved up for the writing process. You need to stimulate your spirit and heart first.

Maybe you're writing a twenty-first-century legal thriller, but you're attracted to a late nineteenth-century surrealist painting of a man levitating over a church at night before a full moon. It doesn't matter if your brain can't make the connection. That picture goes up on the wall. Later it may be that the feelings you picked up from that fanciful painting come into play when the protagonist recalls a childhood memory, but don't worry about that now. Just put up the picture.

A certain picture might remind you of an action sequence—a woman jumping from a window makes you think of your hero tricking his partner. Not literally, but it has the same energy. Or a certain photo might make you think of your novel's period of history—a turn-of-the-century team of men building a bridge. Doesn't matter if your book's about building Roman roads in 300 B.C. Or a certain painting might feel symbolic of one of your themes—a shepherd holds down a nymph, like the men in a small 1920s town keeping their wives from city hall meetings. Whatever appeals to you—it should go up on your display board.

While writing a novel I often pause and punch a few keys on my PC to go online and find images. What the port of Nagasaki looked like in 1918. If you have a color printer, this may be a great way for you to gather visuals.

Some of you will make a display and get nothing from it. It might even make you feel uncomfortable. It's probably because your brain got in the way. You need to follow your bliss, like a dowser divining for water. Look at each image you've gathered and ask yourself, "Does this picture make me happy?" or, "Does this picture feel right?" If the answer isn't yes, then take it down. It's all about gut reaction. Not logic.

USING MUSIC

If a picture paints a thousand words, music paints a thousand pictures. There are layers of emotion in music, just as there should be layers of emotion in your story. Listening to my "writing music" is so helpful to me that when I lived in a hotel for two and a half weeks during a recent move, I packed my bulky stereo in the trunk of my car, brought it up to my room on a luggage rack, and set it up on the tiny table in my hotel room. I use my writing tapes (yes, I still have cassette tapes) so much they're starting to wear out. But my writing music puts me into the mood of my current novel faster than anything else and reminds me to make the characters and scenes and paragraphs and sentences and word choices true, beautiful, strong, and memorable.

Making a Soundtrack

For each writing project I put together a soundtrack, a collection of music to fit the story. In general I'm gathering music that makes me think of those characters and situations, but more specifically, I'm hunting for music that gets at the underlying truth. It's fun and interesting to use music that calls to mind a certain period of history and a certain place on earth, but for me the most important thing is finding music that speaks to the real emotion driving the novel. A story about boxing that involves violence and anger may, at its core, be about love. A horror story may have regret as its inner emotion. A love story might have a beautiful sacrifice hiding underneath.

When describing the way I choose writing music at a workshop I taught, I showed a movie clip where the music underscoring the scene was unexpected yet perfect. In the 1951 film *Scrooge*, as Ebenezer Scrooge arrives at his nephew's house unannounced near the end of the story, he is greeted at the door by a young maid. He is hesitant to enter the drawing room where it is apparent a party is going on; he can hear two guests singing a duet. He is afraid and nearly changes his mind and turns back, but the young maid kindly nods encouragement to him, and he walks through the door. The singers are a young man and woman who stop abruptly as everyone in the room turns to see who has arrived.

Because it's Christmas day, we would expect the duet to be a Christmas carol or hymn, but the song is "Barbara Allen," an old folk song all English children would have recognized, a song about love and regret. This is the perfect choice of music because Scrooge has recently visited his childhood and he regrets all the mistakes he's made in his life. He mourns the loss of his true love as well as his sister's death. At the same time, he is a changed man now. He has come to ask forgiveness. He's regained his ability to love.

This is the way you should choose music—find pieces that feel right, even if they don't seem logical. Robert Frost once said, "A poem is never a put-up job, so to speak. It begins as a lump in the throat, a sense of wrong, a homesickness, a love sickness. It is never a thought to begin with." That's how music works for me—it jumps past the words and the thoughts and stabs at the soul.

I don't usually compose my soundtrack so that the beginning represents the opening scenes of the novel and the last pieces of music represent the last chapter, because it takes a thousand hours to write the novel and only one to play through the soundtrack. For this reason I gather music that overall expresses the feelings of the whole novel.

I tend to choose music without lyrics and mostly from film scores. Some of my favorites are (with the composer): *The Mission* by Ennio Morricone (adventurous, strange, wondrous); *Chocolat* by Rachel Portman (playful, magical, mysterious); *Sense and Sensibility* by Patrick Doyle (sorrowful, hopeful); *Rob Roy* by Carter Burwell (noble, romantic); and *The Englishman Who Went Up a Hill But Came Down a Mountain* by Stephen Endelman (peculiar, delightful, touching). I own dozens of scores. There are some from which I extracted only one track, but I love those tracks and have played them countless times.

More tips for making your own novel soundtrack:

1. Start your soundtrack with the piece of music that sounds the most like the mood of your story, the best fit. This will act as your theme.

2. Make sure none of your selections get cut off. There should be nothing distracting in the flow. The tracks should follow each other with smooth transitions.

3. Try to make the last piece of music on the sound-track be one that ends gently. You want to be writing along, on a run, and not even notice the soundtrack has ended. It's fine to start the music over, but it's also nice to be so carried away that everything except your writing disappears.

Recommended Listening

Here's a list of some of my favorite soundtracks:

- *The Others* by Alejandro Amenabar: strange, dangerous, and anguished

- *Ladies in Lavender* by Nigel Hess: romantic, pure, and charming

- *Kingdom of Heaven* by Harry Gregson-Williams: stark, passionate, and enchanted

- *Hamlet* by Patrick Doyle: honorable, aching, and pensive

- *Gladiator* by Hans Zimmer and Lisa Gerrard: Celtic, rueful, and heroic

- *The Lord of the Rings: The Fellowship of the Ring* by Howard Shore: ethereal, nostalgic, and ominous

- *Carnivàle* by Jeff Beal: bleak, desolate, tender, and eerie

- *Titanic* by James Horner: haunting, sweet, and grand

- *Henry V* by Patrick Doyle: courtly, noble, and pastoral

- *Munich* by John Williams: ancient, holy, and heartbreaking

ADDITIONAL INSPIRATIONS

I'm not shy about using anything I can find that inspires me to get into the emotion of my current novel faster: wearing a certain hand lotion that (for whatever reason) smells like the garden setting in my story, lighting candles if my story takes place before electric lights, drinking tea from a cup and saucer if it reminds me of my Norfolk family. Don't hesitate to utilize whatever tools get you in touch with the mood of your story, even if it seems weird. No one ever has to know. (Although agents and editors love those quirky tidbits when it comes to publicity.) All that counts is that you tap into your novel's emotions.

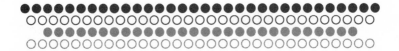

Fun Stuff

- Blindly choose a CD from every category of music at your public library and give them a listen. You might be surprised by what sings to you.

- Walk down the art history aisle at your public library and pull down books randomly. Flip through them until you find a picture that inspires you.

CHAPTER 9

WHAT TO DO WHEN IT STINKS

I try to leave out the parts that people skip.
—Elmore Leonard

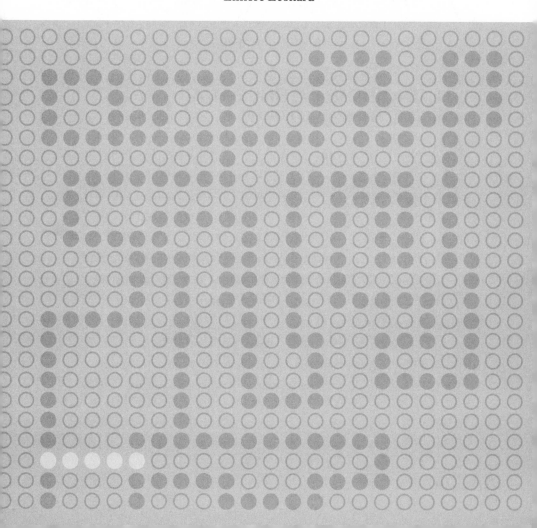

What if you finish your whole manuscript and look back and don't like it? Even worse, what if you don't know why you don't love it? Maybe it needs trimming, but you can't see where, because it's three hundred flippin' pages long. Maybe the voice you started with inspired you but it lapsed into a neutral tone somewhere along the way. Maybe your characters, who began quirky and original, got lost in the action. How discouraging and depressing. The manuscript is horrible and the idea of rewriting it seems devastating.

Take heart. There are some sensible ways of avoiding this situation. What you need is a warning system for sensing trouble, like an alarm that goes off when you stray from the golden road, the perfect version of your novel.

HONOR THE INSTINCT THAT SOMETHING'S OFF

When you sense that you've gotten off track and that the words you are currently writing are not good enough, follow your gut instincts. Stop and look at the sentences one at a time, starting with the last one you wrote. Okay, that one's not quite right. Go back another sentence. Still it doesn't feel right. Go back another sentence and another until you find the last really good sentence. Now look at what came after it, the bad parts. What made it stink? This may have an obvious answer, but it may not.

If you can tell what's wrong, put it on a back burner so you'll recognize that same mistake faster if it crops up again. If you don't know what's wrong with it, that's okay, too. Either way, cut the passage that wasn't good enough and paste it into a document called "Extra Stuff" or "Things I Cut." (It's interesting to reread these parts. Sometimes they contain bits of stuff you can salvage later in the draft or even in another novel.) Now start writing fresh from the end of your last high-quality sentence.

How the Previous Chapters Can Assist You

Things that were discussed in chapters one through eight can help you get back on track.

1. Review the core of your novel, the reason you wanted to write it in the first place.

2. Look at your storytelling device to get some perspective on the whole project.

3. Look at the crosshairs nearest the place you stopped writing for perspective on that chapter.

4. Try a "Shortcut to the Scene" exercise for the passage where you got stuck.

5. Check to make sure you are writing a scene where a scene should be, summarizing a passage that should be summary, or placing reflection where it will work well.

6. Review your outline or your plot diagrams, timeline, and plot menus.

7. Read a similar scene written by one of your favorite authors, one you would like to emulate.

8. Put on some inspiring music and close your eyes, picturing the scene where you got stuck in its *perfect* form—fantasize it as if you were watching the brilliant movie of your novel. Get back in touch with the deeper emotion.

Recommended Reading

- *The Writer's Digest Handbook of Novel Writing*: "Finish That Novel Before It Finishes You" by Raymond Obstfeld

- *Stein on Writing* by Sol Stein: Chapter thirty-two, "Triage: A Better Way of Revising Fiction"

COMMON THINGS THAT GO WRONG WITH ...

Character

1. A character who started out realistic becomes a cartoon stereotype.

2. A character who started out colorful becomes ordinary or dull.

3. A character who started out dynamic loses her oomph and ceases to drive the plot.

4. A character has turned into someone else or is no longer behaving in character.

5. The character arc climaxes too soon so that the protagonist does all her growing only near the beginning of the novel. Or, vice versa, the character arc does not rise at all so that no change takes place until the last moments of the story when it's basically too late.

6. The character is a one-note wonder who only expresses a single emotion throughout the book (only anger, only longing, only fear).

7. Readers don't get emotionally involved with a major character.

8. The character is not appealing enough.

9. The character is a knockoff, and so seems unreal.

10. There are too many characters to get invested in any one of them.

Plot

1. The plot is not original enough; it feels like a formula we've seen a thousand times.

2. The readers always know exactly what's going to happen; They're always three steps ahead;

3. The plot is boring.

4. It's all action so that the frenzied story numbs the readers.

5. It's too complex.

6. It's too shallow; there is not enough substance.

7. Suspension of disbelief is destroyed because the setup for an unbelievable event was insufficient.

8. Too many subplots make the plot overly complex; it's boring because the readers space out.

9. The sequence is too illogical to follow.

10. The premise is not compelling.

11. The conclusion is unsatisfying.

Setting

1. The setting is not sufficiently described so the readers can't picture it.

2. The setting is described well, but it's not an interesting place.

3. It's too dark.

4. It's not dark enough, or not dark at all.

5. The setting is too complex to imagine.

6. There is only one setting, and it's not amazing enough to sustain a whole novel.

7. The setting is incorrect for the story.

8. The setting feels lifted from another story.

Theme

1. The theme is inconsistent.

2. It's a non-truth.

3. It's too preachy.

4. It's too obvious.

5. There are too many themes.

6. The theme doesn't fit the story.

Backstory and Exposition

1. The backstory or exposition is too blatant.

2. The exposition comes too late in the story.

3. There is too much of it at once.

4. The backstory is repeated.

5. Some of the backstory or exposition is missing.

6. The exposition is corny, cliché, or melodramatic.

7. It is too familiar.

8. It is irrelevant to the story.

9. It is inconsistent.

Language

1. The language is too simple.

2. It's overly highbrow.

3. It's wrong for the character or narrating voice.

4. It's inconsistent.

5. Words are stolen from another work.

6. Words are difficult to sound out or there are too many foreign words.

7. Words are underexplained or overexplained.

8. The language is boring.

Voice/Tone

1. The voice or tone is too light.

2. It's too dark.

3. It's inconsistent.

4. It's not striking enough.

5. It's too familiar; it feels like a spoof.

6. There is not enough emotion.

7. The tone lacks tension.

Pacing and Structure

1. The pacing makes the manuscript read like two different books.

2. The pace is too slow.

3. The pace is too fast.

4. There is too much or too little denouement.

5. The acts are unbalanced.

The Device

1. The device doesn't fit the story.

2. It is started and then is dropped.

3. It doesn't come in until too late in the story.

4. The device uses the wrong props.

5. It's too blatant.

6. It's too familiar.

7. The device is mixed with another.

FIXING COMMON THINGS THAT GO WRONG WITH …

Character

1. A character who started out realistic becomes a cartoon stereotype. Look back in your manuscript and reread the first, or best, example of the character's personality on display, the most telling passage you wrote about him in his realistic, gritty glory. Then look back at every unrealistic and cartoonish moment your wrote for him. Mark the passages and rewrite them with that best sample of this character's behavior in mind.

2. A character who started out colorful becomes ordinary or dull. Backtrack and find every boring passage you inadvertently wrote for this character. Mark them. Then aanswer two questions for every ordinary passage, something like this: *What would Jane never do at a dinner party with her boss? She'd never agree with everyone and keep the peace. What would she actually do at a dinner party with her boss? She'd actually bring up touchy subjects, tell an overly intimate story about herself, and spill something.* You'll know how to rewrite the passage better after coming up with these "he would never" and "he would probably" answers.

3. A character who started out dynamic loses her oomph and ceases to drive the plot. Look at every turning point in the manuscript so far. In the beginning your protagonist is probably driving the plot. Mark the places where she is not. Then make a list of possible actions she could take that would move the plot forward. If one or more of your new ideas takes the plot in a different direction than you anticipated, be open-minded. It might be better than your original idea.

4. A character has turned into someone else or is no longer behaving in character. First look to see if the person your character morphed into isn't a better idea. If not, backtrack to the place where you feel that character jumped the track. It was probably something else in the story that made you skip off the path. Did you feel the scene needed to be funny and your character was too serious as originally created? Did you think the tone of the book was getting too light so you tried to push your fanciful character into dark moods? Did you think the storyline needed some heroics? Did you turn your antihero into a hero by accident? Find that first out-of-character page and rewrite the pages after it by first writing in the margins a list of the unnatural behavior next to the more character-appropriate behavior: "comforts brother but should ignore brother" or "hides evidence but should help cops follow clues."

5. The character arc climaxes too soon or does not rise at all. Write an outline of just the growth of that character, a character arc, and shape those things into a nice three-act structure: act one (first 25 percent or so of the story), the character is drawn into the plot; act two (second 50 percent), things become more difficult; and act three (last 25 percent), the character is driven to a climax, changes in a vital way. Look at the best map for that character's emotional progress ,and then see if you can fit it into the logical plot map of the action in the story. Could your character not actually conquer her fears until act three? Could she be bold enough to forgive her mother in act one when she needs to leave home and go off on her adventure?

6. The character is a one-note wonder. So your main character feels the same way for too long, and it's starting to get boring. Make a list of other emotions, the one's he is not feeling so far, and how those emotions might be stirred by the plot, setting, or other characters. If your environmental-ist is angry all the time at the politicians and factory owners, perhaps she could also be frightened by contamination, disgusted by test results, guilty about not starting the good fight sooner, pleased at a small victory, or confused by her family's or friends' reaction to her plight.

7. Readers don't get emotionally involved with a major character. You may feel a character is accessible because you know everything about him. Then you are confused when you give your critique group members or friends or family your manuscript to read and they say they had trouble feeling for the protagonist. This gap between the character and readers is not uncommon, but it's not as hard to fix as you might think. Make a list of everything wonderful about this character: brave, thoughtful, smart, vulnerable, etc. Then, for each term, write three ways this quality could be shown to the reader. *Brave—jumps in the river to save the dog, walks right into the loan shark's office, let's his ex-wife blame him for their daughter's broken arm even though it was not his fault.* When you list a characteristic and can't find the place in the story where the readers get a view of it, you'll know where to start rewriting.

8. The character is not appealing enough. Maybe the character is too shallow, too selfish, not nice enough. This is a tricky problem if you want the character to be interesting but not likable. It can work, but you need to make sure he is written in such real detail that the readers feel they are in that character's skin. Charles Dickens pulls this off in *A Christmas Carol* because Scrooge quickly becomes a terrified fish out of water and is exposed to painful memories. Patricia

Highsmith makes Tom in *The Talented Mr. Ripley* a completely compelling sociopath because the readers hear every thought in his unusual head. Soon readers are trying to help him think up ways to get away with murder.

If you are writing a character who is meant to be appealing but she has come out unappealing, it's simpler. Write out everything positive or endearing this character has done so far in the story. *She has helped her boyfriend clear up the breakfast dishes, fed her cat before leaving for work, said hello to the mailman.* Now make a list of everything she has done that could feel negative, especially to an outside reader. *She has had bad thoughts about her ex-husband's new girlfriend, coveted her boss's parking space, been annoyed at the tech guy who couldn't retrieve her lost document.* The negative list may be longer, or contain more powerful messages, than the positive list. How can you transform those negative things? I'm not trying to tell you to write perfect characters or a sappy story. Characters need to be flawed. But sometimes a slight twist on a negative action can help the readers feel empathy for the character and like them enough to keep reading about them.

9. The character is a knockoff, and so seems unreal. If you're patterning a character after another famous character— a Han Solo type, a Scarlett O'Hara type, a Pee-wee Herman type—you might be painting them too close to the original portrait. If you're afraid this is what's going wrong with your story, take a step back and list those qualities in the famous character that attracted you to him. Just because you want your protagonist to be as self-assured as Han Solo or as childlike and playful as Pee-wee doesn't mean, for instance, that he needs to speak with the same vocabulary, dress the same, look the same as the character you're honoring. Take only the most important feature from the original and make most of the other aspects of your character different to guarantee no comparisons.

10. There are too many characters to get invested in. Often an easy way to cut down on characters (and simplify the story) is to combine a few of the less important ones. If yor hero confides in a best friend, ask legal advice from a lawyer, or goes to a doctore when he's been a fight and needs patching up, have all three be the same person (best friend who's a lawyer and knows first aid). Or if you have four girlfriends for your protagonist, perhaps choose two.

Plot

1. The plot is not original enough. Go back through the pages and highlight anything you see that you've read in another book or seen in a movie. In the margin, write where you've seen it before. Then list these sections and make a note for each one on how it could differ from its look-alike. A mental patient escapes by throwing something heavy through a window. *Too much like* One Flew Over the Cuckoo's Nest? *Instead the patient walks out with a visiting grandma convincing her he's an old friend.* Quick notes like these can help you detach from unintentional imitation.

2. Readers always know exactly what's going to happen. This may happen because you've chosen a plot point that's overused or because you keep giving away the answer.

Readers know the villain is going to whip out a picture of the hero's son and blackmail her by pretending to have kidnapped the little boy because you showed the villain taking pictures of the child and driving away from the schoolyard. You could be less obvious by only showing the antagonist sitting in the car watching the boy on the playground and no more.

3. The plot is boring. Take each page and imagine what different writers might do with the same piece of plot. Choose extreme examples. Would a comedy writer have the cab driver and the villain coincidentally be childhood friends with unfinished business? Would the mystery writer have the taxi pass a clue on a street corner that makes a new connection for the hero? Would the horror writer have the cab driver channel a ghost? It doesn't matter if these ideas don't fit your story. You're not going to use them. But often, after thinking of ideas to make the story more interesting and exciting that you're not going to use, you begin to come up with workable ideas that are just as stimulating but better suited to your book. Or imagine what would be the most surprising thing that could happen in a given scene, the last thing the reader would suspect.

4. The plot is all action so that the frenzied pace numbs the readers. Let them breathe. Give the readers a little downtime now and then in your action story. Look back at your favorite action novels. Notice the conversations, summarized passages, meals, introspection, release of emotions that are set in between the car chases, shoot-outs, and confrontations.

List them. Give the readers a chance to breathe now and then in your own manuscript. Find the dramatic respites that come from your characters' needs, flaws, and strengths.

5. The plot is too complex. Often a complex plot can be trimmed into a sleek one by cutting out some steps. Does your protagonist have to visit her father in the hospital twice, once to bring him flowers and talk about Mom and the next day to find he has taken a turn for the worse? Couldn't he take a turn for the worse while she's still there the first time? Does your villain need to have three motives for revenge? Would one or two be interesting enough? Does your antihero have to have a plan A that fails and a plan B that works? Could you skip plan A? To find the messiness in your overly complex story, tell it out loud to yourself in summary. When a section takes too long to explain, make a note. When you find yourself saying, "Oh, wait, I forgot to mention that ..." you're probably in need of a plot trim. When deciding whether to simplify the plot, ask yourself over and over again, "Why does she do that? Why didn't she just do this?" Making a plot less complicated does not have to make it less clever. I'm all for clever twists and needing to use my brain when I read a great novel. The simplification should be only for trimming unnecessary muck. You're not making it plain as in dull. You're making it clear.

6. The plot is too shallow. Sometimes as writers we get caught up in the action. The symbolism. The metaphors. The witty dialogue. The great character names. The slick descriptions. Sometimes we ride these skills over the surface of the story and forget what's really important. If you, or your first readers (friends, family, agent), complain that the novel feels insubstantial, step back and ask yourself these questions: Why am I bothering to write this story? Why does the outcome matter to the characters? How do the characters change? If it ended differently for them, would it make any difference in their world? How did my favorite book affect me the first time I read it?

7. Suspension of disbelief is destroyed. Readers need to buy into the reality put forward by the novel they're reading. You may go too far with a plot point or not far enough with preparing your audience for that plot point. If you have something happen in the book that sounded right when you outlined it but is coming off as farfetched even to you, look back at the stepping-stones that led to the event. If your protagonist steps through a window and goes back in time in chapter nine, make sure chapter one prepares the readers for the kind of story they will be reading and make sure chapters two through eight gradually set up a reality that will sustain a time-travel element. If your murderer turns over a new leaf at the end of act two, make sure you've given her reason to. Look back and repave the road leading up to your sharp turn.

8. Too many subplots make the plot overly complex. If you start to feel weighed down by your numerous storylines, start cutting them. List the subplots (shopkeeper with a crush, neighbor's dog that tears up the garden, accountant that threatens to quit every day), and then list under each point all reasons it is necessary. Only subplots that are so vital that you could not remove them without destroying your novel get to stick around. Be bold. Cut away.

9. The sequence is illogical. Sometimes the sequence set down in an outline starts to show its true colors when you're writing the chapters. If you feel the order of scenes or events in your story is off, go back to your outline cards (those 3" × 5" cards where you wrote each scene on a separate card so you could easily rearrange them) and, in red ink, write a question mark on every card that doesn't feel right where it is in the old outline. Shuffle the cards. I'm not kidding. Mix them up completely. When you lay them out again in the order you think they might work best, give special attention to those with red question marks. Something about these scenes tricked you the first time. This time really look closely at the proper place for those tricky bits.

10. The premise is not compelling. If what feels wrong with your book is a wimpy premise, it is hoped you'll sniff it out right away. It's hard on a writer to complete a first draft and decide that what stinks is the main idea of the book. If you fear that a mediocre premise is your holdup, take out a sheet of paper. Write a list on the left-hand side of the paper of everything that's dodgy about your present premise. Then write a list down the right-hand side of the page about all the things that work great in the premise of a similar favorite book, play, or movie. See where you might make the risks higher, the characters more emotional, the setting more a part of the plot. The premise should make your readers curious.

11. The conclusion is unsatisfying. If you feel the ending to your story is weak, do the same for the conclusion or climax of your novel as you did for the premise. Write a list of what bothers you about your conclusion and next to it a list of what worked great about the end of your favorite novel. Do you have to create more suspense before you give the readers what they've been craving? Do you need to make the answer to the mystery clearer? Does the villain need to be angrier or perhaps show remorse? Unsatisfying conclusions are usually lacking something or don't have enough of that something. Whatever that is, make your story's ending have *more* of it.

Setting

1. The setting is not sufficiently described. You, as the writer, may see your novel's setting in great detail in your head, but you have not been giving the readers enough to see clearly. If you feel this about your manuscript, take novels off your shelves or wander the stacks at the public library or in the aisle of a bookstore, and flip random books open. Scan for descriptions. Read and observe how self-confident writers can be about their descriptions. They freely give away the scents, textures, sounds, hues of light. No need for you to be stingy with the pen. Take one of your shortest descriptive passages and force yourself to write it three times as long.

2. The setting is described well, but it's not an interesting place. So you feel comfortable with the length of your descriptions; it's the content that doesn't feel right. Make two lists for the passage of description that's worrying you: the details that matter and those that don't. Now, only shop from the list that matters. Here's an example for a description of the family graveyard: *Doesn't matter—Groundskeeper's name,*

jet trail in sky, name of street the cemetery is on. Does mat-
ter—Wife's grave is the only one with flowers, a tree seems to
shade her headstone in a protective way, a mouse chooses to
sit on her grave rather than any of the others. Cut every un-
interesting phrase from your descriptions and replace them
with the kinds of details that make the picture you're painting
more effective.

3. The setting is too dark. If you feel your setting is suffering from an unintended darkness, go back and highlight
every sentence, phrase, or word that sounds too heavy. Use
this guideline to rewrite a lighter version of the setting. It may
be as simple as a handful of words.

4. The setting is not dark enough. You may feel your setting is unrealistically sunny. Reread your descriptions, making a check mark in the margins when you feel you might have
an opportunity to bring in some dimension that mirrors the
main problem of your plot, that foreshadows a future mishap,
or that gives your setting some darker shades of meaning.

5. The setting is too complex to imagine. The setting has
so many features (rooms, streets, offices, machines, desks,
bridges) that the readers need a map to keep them straight. If
you start to get a headache from your overly complicated setting choices, first ask yourself these two questions: *Is the setting*
itself too complicated for the story? Or is the manner in which I
am describing it or using it unclear? If the setting is too obtuse
for the story, break it down into its most essential features. If
it's the way you bring in the setting that confounds, highlight
all the sentences in your manuscript that describe the setting,

write them on cards, and place them in order of importance. The setting of the haunted house may require the hall mirror and the koi pond and the shed with the locked trunk because they are important to the plot, but maybe it doesn't need the dumbwaiter, the chapel, the dressing room, and the fifty-two other extraneous features you've included for color.

6. There is only one setting, and it's not enough to sustain a whole novel. Sometimes a single setting can carry you through a whole book, but it's rare. Unless there's something fascinating and brilliant about your use of a single setting (a lifeboat, a padded cell, the apartment of an agoraphobic), try to give your readers some variety. Even if you were writing a haunted house mystery where the protagonist is an artist who works at home, she would usually still be better off visiting the store or her friend's apartment, a pub, her psychologist's office. Think of some logical alternate locations in which some of the action can take place.

7. The setting is incorrect for the story. Sometimes you just choose the wrong setting for your story and you have to figure it out by trial and error. If the setting feels fake, a bad fit, close your eyes and picture your characters. Where would they look right? Picture a key slice of the action. What would be the best backdrop for this scene? Don't worry if your instincts tell you that a bakery is better than a college faculty lounge—just try it.

8. The setting feels lifted from another story. If you have taken to the setting in some other writer's novel, play, or movie and it's starting to show, don't panic. You can go back and tweak it with originality. Highlight all the descriptions of the setting. Now change every word that is a giveaway as to your inspiration. It may still look like the Great Hall at Hogwarts or Jerry Seinfeld's apartment in your head, but it doesn't have to sound that way on the page.

Theme

1. The theme is inconsistent. If the theme you started with seems to have taken on a life of its own and run away on a tangent, don't force it back on your original path. First try to figure out why it jumped the tracks. Did it start out "war is bad" and end up "war is necessary"? Or did it start out "love is what it's all about" and turn into "be true to yourself"? Look at where you landed and decide whether this is actually the better concept. If you slipped with the theme, your subconscious may be trying to guide you. After all, it's not as if someone else convinced you to switch. Your own writing took you there. Rethink the core of your story. Keep an open mind.

2. The theme is a non-truth. As you are writing you may start to disbelieve your own theme. "War is necessary?" you begin to say to yourself. "I don't think so." Again, take a step back and recall the best thing in your story, that core of wonder that made it impossible for you not to write this book. What does it tell you about your theme?

3. The theme is too preachy. One of the worst and one of the easiest things to do is overindulge your message. It's good to have a theme, but be subtle. Gently weave it into the story. No soapboxes, unless your character truly is that kind of fanatic. If you're being too heavy with your theme, go back and smooth it into the story. You'll be surprised how fast it improves the manuscript.

4. The theme is too obvious. Duh! Does your theme have zero controversy? Let's say you've chosen the theme "loneliness is painful." The readers may think your story is a bit obvious. Expand on the theme a little to add dynamics to your tale. "Loneliness is painful" might become "loneliness is in the eye of the beholder."

5. There are too many themes. Having too many themes eventually has as much impact as having none because the symbolism, irony, and allegories become a muddle. Stick to one or a few. Backtrack and choose only your most powerful images, illustrations, and allusions.

6. The theme doesn't fit the story. As with an inconsistent theme, go back and look at your novel's core. If the theme doesn't seem to fit, try not thinking about it for a few chapters. See what grows.

Backstory and Exposition

1. The backstory or exposition is too blatant. I hate exposition that sounds fake and forced. If you start to feel your writing stinks because of the way you're trying to squeeze in backstory, stop. Go find your favorite novel and reread the first chapter. Write down everything you learned about the story, the setting, the characters, in the first few pages. I'm guessing your favorite novel didn't need to resort to dialogue like this: "Hey, Stella. Don't worry. You dropped out of high school at fifteen, had a baby at sixteen, brought up a daughter by yourself, worked two jobs for a decade, and took night classes to get your law degree. I'm sure you can handle a simple surprise party." (Ugh.) Look at how your favorite author managed to give the setting, the main characters, and the central conflict without making the readers groan.

2. The exposition comes too late in the story. If you catch the reader up on some essentials late in the game (say, act three), see if you can find a natural (subtle) way of including some of that information earlier. I hate when someone telling me a story absentmindedly adds, "Oh, wait, I forget to tell you that Stan is also a stunt man." I don't think so. It sounds too convenient. Set it up better. It may be easy to insert the right information in an earlier chapter.

3. There is too much exposition at once. Don't be guilty of squashing in too much backstory all at once. List the information you're trying to clump up, then choose which parts of it you can extract and replace in other spots.

4. The backstory is repeated. If you're telling the readers backstory they've already heard (or have inferred because it was implied), trust your instincts. If you're typing on a computer, do word searches for key words in that bit of backstory: "baseball" or "Smith College." See what you've already gone over and pick the best position for it.

5. Some of the backstory or exposition is missing. Something doesn't feel right. It's because you are talking about a character or a plot point for which you have skipped the exposition entirely. Again, let the word search function help you. Find a key word that if you had included the backstory would appear in an earlier chapter. If it's not there, go back and find the perfect place to set it up.

6. The exposition is corny, cliché, or melodramatic. You may feel your writing stinks because you've been including overused ways of summing up backstory. Stop and reread. Highlight any cliché phrases and reword them. No wallflowers, loose cannons, bad apples, or tough cookies. Unless you're writing comedy and are great at it, transform the corn from your exposition. It doesn't take more words to be original, just the right ones. And if the backstory sounds like a joke because it's too melodramatic, look at each point and try to find a way to tone down the description.

7. The backstory is too familiar. As with clichés, if your exposition sounds like the backstory from a well-known book, play, or movie, go back and highlight those phrases that need to be adjusted. Go for the unexpected detail.

8. The backstory and exposition are irrelevant to the story. If you are displeased with your writing because there's too much backstory and exposition, cheer up. It's probably because there's something in there that can be snipped out completely. No need to reword it—just cut it. Any sentence that can be removed without confusing the readers in the long run should be edited out. Go back through and highlight the essential facts, then delete the rest.

9. The backstory is inconsistent. Once in a while you make a simple mistake. You wrote one fact in chapter two and a contradicting fact in chapter thirteen. Hey, this one's easy to fix. You'll probably catch it in your rewrite, but make yourself feel better right now. Go back and look. Maybe you said the villain grew up in Fresno on page twelve and Bakersfield on page twenty-nine. If only all problems were this easy to solve.

Language

1. The language is too simple. One of the more subtle kinds of discomfort writers experience partway through a draft of a novel is the feeling that the voice, the language of the narrator, is too plain for the story. Here's another instance when I feel you should turn to your favorite authors. Who do you want to write like? What novel do you want your reviewers to compare yours to? Read the first ten pages of one of these books. Read out loud. Go back and retell the opening of your novel with this richer, more complex language still in your ear.

2. The language is overly highbrow. On the other hand, you may think you want to write like a certain author, but the vocabulary and sentence structures you are using to get there are totally wrong for the story at hand. In this case, take your opening page and, for contrast, rewrite it in the opposite style. Turn the language of upper-class London into working-class East L.A. Turn science genius into man-of-few-words farmer. Turn poetic diplomat into comedic rebel. It will probably bring the right language choice to mind.

3. The language is wrong for the narrator. Perhaps the language choice you made seems right for the whole story, but it doesn't work for your protagonist. Try reworking it with the language of your hero in mind. Go back and do one of the exercises from chapter two about practicing your narrator's speech patterns. (But keep an open mind. Maybe you chose the wrong character to be your protagonist.)

4. The language is inconsistent. Look for passages where your language fluctuates and mark them. That may be a clue as to which type of language you should stick with. Does one style tend to come in during the more important passages? That may be the better fit. After you know which one is not as appropriate for the story, go back and tweak the other passages for consistency.

5. Words are stolen from another work. If you feel guilty for lifting some unique language from another writer, you're busted. Go back and cut it. Make up your own version of this. No stealing magical terms from Harry Potter or quirky slang from *A Clockwork Orange*. Create your own nouns and expletives.

6. Words are difficult to sound out. Watch out for using too many terms that are difficult to pronounce, long scientific names (*Loxodonta africana* instead of elephant), foreign phrases in every sentence (French beaches Les Sables-d'Olonne and Châtelaillon-Plage), or the spelling-out of characters' accents or baby talk ("toof faiwy" for "tooth fairy"). If these kinds of words or phrases worry you in your manuscript, you've probably already gone too far. Give your readers a break. Cut a few.

7. Words are not explained. You may have used language that you forgot to explain. Read back through and mark every word or phrase that may need an assist. But don't overexplain them. Put in just enough explanation to keep the readers on track without slowing the pace.

8. The language is boring. If you're afraid your writing stinks because the language is boring, buck up! Go back through and start by taking one boring word per paragraph and replacing it with a more exciting one. At first you may be using replacement words that are a bit on the goofy side (not "she ran," "she charged"; not "he passed out," "he swooned"), but before long you will start to feel the natural impulse to choose the more interesting candidates.

Voice/Tone

1. The tone is too light. If you start to worry that your novel's not working because the tone is too light for the story, stop. Reread what you have so far, highlighting the most blatant passages that seem wrong. Start by revising these sections with the voice you hear in your head, the one you compared the bad writing with, the voice that lets you know you were slipping into a false voice. (If you need to, read the first few pages of a favorite novel that has the kind of darker voice you desire.) After adjusting these passages, the voice for the rest of the novel will probably come out better the first time through each scene.

2. The tone is too dark. It's the same as with a tone that is too light. Reread and pull out the sections that are too heavy and shadowed. Revise them first; then the lighter voice you've imagined will start to come more naturally.

3. The voice is inconsistent. Sometimes the voice is too dark, sometimes too light, sometimes too formal or informal, antiquated, or modern and offhand. Create a set of symbols for the potential voice problems: arrow up for too light, arrow down for too heavy or dark, a circle for too informal, a square for too formal, the letters BC for too antiquated, MOD for too modern, and so on. Reread your manuscript, marking the inconsistencies in the voice. Again, choose a novel you love with a consistent voice you would like to emulate. Read a few pages aloud. Then start to revise your manuscript at all the places where you drew symbols in the margins, keeping your favorite author's voice in mind.

4. The tone is not striking enough. If you feel your language is too safe, too ordinary, do what I did with a writer I admire. When I was rewriting *A Certain Slant of Light*, I stopped and took the book *White Oleander* by Janet Fitch and opened it randomly, slapped it on the copier, and then looked at the two pages that came out of the machine. I did this three times. On those six pages I made a notation every time Fitch said something in a striking way, used a poetic metaphor or simile that I'd never heard before, or made a very unusual word choice. She could be startling an average of twice per page. Then I went back to my own manuscript and highlighted all of my striking moments. If a page had no marks, I went back and found some way of using language in a fresh manner. I kept at it until there was no page without a fresh phrase.

5. The tone is too familiar. If the way you use language is too much like a well-known writer, your prose may come off as a kind of spoof. This usually happens when the voice you're writing like is very unusual. If you use convoluted 1920s British slang exactly like P.G. Wodehouse's Bertie Wooster, or if you put together thoughts with the exact same rhythm and expletive choices made by Chuck Palahniuk in *Fight Club*, it will probably be misunderstood and distracting. It's fine to be inspired by another writer's wit and brilliance, but don't mimic. Go back through your manuscript and circle all the "too close for comfort" moments. Then make them more *you*.

6. There is not enough emotion. As described in chapter eight, find music that reminds you of the central emotions in your story. Play this music as you rewrite. If you're still having trouble with a particularly cold scene, do a ten-minute writing on what your characters are feeling. Use all the senses. Let your mind run wild.

7. The tone lacks tension. Look at what is happening in the scene that feels tension free. Make sure that the characters in the scene want different things. They should have mismatched goals. There should always be layers to a scene. It isn't just a family dinner where the daughter asks to borrow the car and is thwarted. The daughter wants to sneak away to meet her lover and is frustrated that she can't wrangle more freedom out of her parents, the mother wants to cover up the daughter's misbehavior and have her husband believe she is in control, the father is disappointed with his daughter and blames his wife. Make sure plenty is going on and that your scenes leave things hanging and unresolved.

Pace and Structure

1. It's like two different books. Contemplative passages can be slower paced than action sequences, but you can't have a book that feels like every other chapter is written by someone else. If your manuscript has an erratic pace, think about why the writing is inconsistent. It could be you need to revise your slow passages when you're feeling upbeat and revise your fast-paced sections when you're feeling grounded and calm.

2. The pace is too slow. If you're worried that your pacing is too sluggish, listen to your instincts. Most manuscripts that feel slow suffer from too many words. (It can also be extraneous scenes, overly complicated plot, too many characters, and so on, but words are usually to blame.) Take one page from your manuscript, one you feel is rougher than most, and cut out every adjective and adverb. Read it back. If it's better without them, leave them out. Or at least choose only to keep the best ones. Does it give you any ideas about how to trim the draft? Another problem could be action that does not flow correctly. If cutting words isn't helping, go back and look at the outline again. There might be plot points put together awkwardly that could be rearranged (or cut) to keep your readers turning the pages.

3. The pace is too fast. Even the most exciting thrillers have to have some dips in intensity. You don't want to wear out your readers or give them headaches. You want them to stay up all night and finish your novel at three A.M. If you're concerned that your pacing has sped out of control, look back at the things that happen just after each climax. Where can you put a short passage of slower-paced material? A conversation reflecting on what has happened, a character struggling with an emotion? A clue the readers can stand still to observe? Watch your favorite action, horror, thriller, or adventure movie and see what falls between the chases, explosions, attacks, hunts, and escapes.

4. The story has the wrong amount of denouement. The denouement, the winding down of the action after the climax, should also be in balance with the rest of the book. If your readers have been with you for 480 pages, a one-page cooldown after an exciting climax will feel like a cheat. On the other hand, a forty-page cooldown at the end of a novel that is only two hundred pages long will be dreadfully anticlimactic. Think of it this way: Your readers need to be prepared to say goodbye to your characters. Give them a scene, or a few scenes, to discover what's to become of your protagonist, how your antagonist will get away or be punished, how your subplots resolve. If your denouement seems short, list your storylines and see if you've left anyone dangling. If your denouement seems excessive, reread it and take out anything that doesn't show an emotion, a resolution, a farewell, or a reaction to the story's end. Or take out anything you don't love. Never answer a question your readers are not asking.

5. The acts are unbalanced. Usually the first act of a novel presents the problem and engages the main characters, the second builds the story and becomes more complicated (including raising the stakes and twists in the plot), and the third act brings the story to a climax and includes the winding down of the action and the tying off of loose ends. So if the three acts are already so different, what do I mean by unbalanced? Some off-balance stories spend 90 percent of their pages on the first act, all setup and exposition. Some spend 90 percent on the action-packed third act. The most common act imbalance is the weak, short, or even nonexistent second act. If you think this might be your problem, on a piece of paper write down a very short description of what happens in each chapter, one sentence per chapter. Then draw lines that show where the act breaks are. Where is the turning point that takes you into act two? The hero is committed to the hunt, and the action rises. Where is the end of act two? There should be a turning point where things get more serious—a comrade is lost, a sidekick deserts the cause; it's a whole different ball game. If your acts are out of proportion, review your crosshairs, your big moments. If you have to, redo the outline cards for your story.

The Device

1. The device doesn't fit the story. As I mentioned in chapter two, you'll probably sense if you're trying to fit your story into the wrong device. Your first question should be: *Do I even need a device?* The second question should be: *What* *alternate shape does the story want to take?* What does that tell you about the nature of your story? Nothing's worse than a strained storytelling device. Try another one. Try letting the story go device free.

2. The device is started and then is dropped. You sense trouble because you started out with a certain device (journal, book of wisdom, ode), then you found you dropped it out completely. Answer these questions: *Should the device even be there? Does the story call for some other kind of device?*

3. It comes too late in the story. Perhaps you didn't get the swing of using your device until act two. Not to worry. Look at your favorite passage so far, the best example of the proper use of your device. Now go back to page one of your manuscript, reading forward, and write notes in the margins of ways you might insert the device in the same fashion used in your ideal example.

4. The device uses the wrong props. You love your choice of a storytelling device, but something about the way you're applying it is making you fall out of love with your novel. Could be the props. They have to match the device. Otherwise it will just be a mess. A documentary does not have confessions in it. A diary will probably not be laced with lessons in wisdom. Make sure you're not trimming your manuscript with the props from a device you're not employing.

5. The device is too blatant. You might start to feel dissatisfied with your writing if your device is too obvious. Let's say, for example, you chose a cookbook device which at first seemed cool, but soon you got tired of the recipe chapter openers and now your narration is starting to sounds like this: *When he added the stinging salt of cruelty to the beaten eggs of her broken heart, she felt whipped, grilled, burned, and left out to dry.* Okay, that was a silly example, but you get the idea. If your device is strangling your story, toss it or tone it down. With a heavy-handed device, it might be good to cut all of it out temporarily, tone down the ideas in a brainstorming session, and then try reinserting a little at a time to see how it feels. Better to have no device than a distractingly blatant one.

6. The device is too familiar. It's fine to use a device that's been used before, but if your story is too similar to a story that used the same device, critics and fans will not be gentle. If you're writing about an English girl who's trying to lose weight, cut down on her drinking, quit smoking, and stop flirting with her boss, don't use the diary device. If what's making you dislike your manuscript is a fear of being a copycat, google your subject matter and device. "Novel diary diet boss" or "haunted house novel documentary" or "fiction letters teen cocaine." Chances are you'll be fine, but if the device you're using makes you nervous, there may be a reason. One good way to check on possible look-alikes is to ask your local librarian or bookstore clerk, *"Do you know a horror novel that's told like a vampire's book report?"* If they can't think of one, you're probably in the clear.

7. It's a mixed device. You started with a documentary and it morphed into a journal? You started with an ode and it ended up with a fairy tale? First decide which device is a better fit. Was the first half of the manuscript working better or the last half? Then retrace your steps, forward or back, from the page of departure. If the problem is that you switched back and forth throughout, highlight the uses of the device that you want to extract or transform. Adjust each guilty passage one at a time.

EXERCISE: WHY IT WORKS/ WHY IT DOESN'T

When I was in high school, my sister Cynthia was just beginning her screenwriting career. We would write together, not on the same project, just in the same room, at opposite ends of our family dining room table. She worked on movie scripts, and I worked on my first attempt at a novel. We became movie buddies—we'd watch movies and TV shows and plays together and pick them apart. When we loved them, we would go over every detail that made that script great. We'd discuss why those stories worked. When we didn't like movies or plays, we'd pick them apart in frustration. We'd list our complaints and talk about why those moments didn't work. We'd play the "here's what would've been better" game.

Do the same thing now with the scene you're not happy with in your own novel. Complain about your own writing. What about it bugs you, annoys you, disappoints you? Now say, "Here's what would've been better," and write *that*.

FIXING THINGS LATER

Even though we have talked about all the ways of getting down a great draft of your novel the first time around, it won't be perfect. And that's okay. Even after all of this preparation and all of these exercises and shortcuts, you will probably have rewriting to do. And you'll feel fine about it, because *you can still go back and fix things later.* Don't let the fear of writing crap slow you down. If embracing this truth helps you relax and lets your writing flow, embrace the hell out it. YOU CAN FIX THINGS LATER! And no one needs to see your first draft but you.

Fun Stuff

- Write a fictional e-mail to a friend or family member as if you're done with your novel. What will you say? How will you feel?

- Make a list of what you'll do the day after you finish your draft. Go to the movies, clean out the garage, sleep in until noon, go fishing. And know that that day will be here soon.

CHAPTER 10

GOALS AND MIRACLES

*I only write when I'm inspired, so I see to it that
I'm inspired every morning at nine o'clock.*

—Peter De Vries

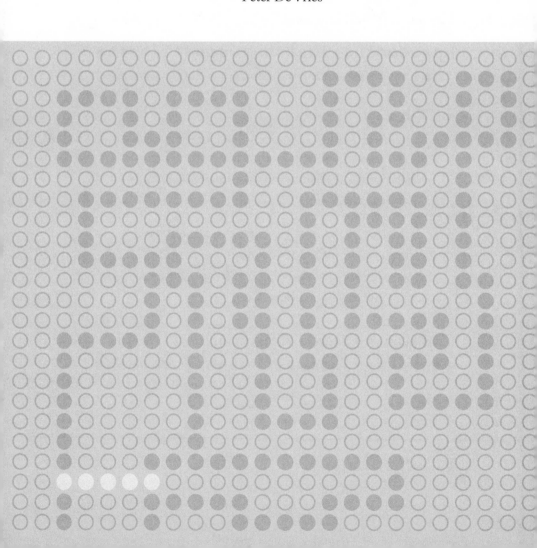

The best incentive for completing and turning in a manuscript is the deadline for which your publisher has paid you in advance. But there are other ways to motivate you to finish a draft fast.

ESTABLISHING A ROUTINE

If you get in the habit of writing at a certain time every day for a set number of minutes or hours, you'll train yourself to be more productive. Whether you have a free schedule or work full time, decide on a writing routine for yourself: You'll write every evening after dinner instead of watching TV. You'll get up an hour earlier and write before going to work. You'll skip playing online bridge and write during your lunch hour instead.

Some writers set an amount of writing to complete per day, rather than an amount of time to fill with writing. I have a friend who makes sure he produces a thousand words a day. That's four pages. That could be a whole scene. Whether you set realistic goals (an hour of writing before bed; three pages before dinner) or imagine fabulous miracles (I want fifty pages this weekend), you need to celebrate the great writing days and not stress the nonwriting days. No matter the seriousness or close proximity of my deadlines, there will always be some days when no writing happens at all. When this happens to you, don't beat yourself up just get back in there tomorrow and write.

SELF-IMPOSED DEADLINES

The trick to giving yourself a deadline is to make it solid by affixing it to something that can't be altered. If you simply say,

"I'll give myself until the end of September," there's really nothing keeping you from saying, "Or maybe by Halloween. Or for sure Thanksgiving." It works better if you attach your finish line to an immovable date.

Decide to finish the manuscript by April 3 because you're leaving for a week-long family vacation the next day. Or choose to finish by the first week in August because a friend has agreed to read it for you while she's on a cruise and she sails on August 8.

You could give yourself a deadline of a writing contest, but I personally would not send off a first draft, no matter how much I loved it, to any contest (except a 3-Day Novel Contest) without plenty of time to polish it. But if you feel this is the best kind of deadline for you, do it.

You can also make interim, self-imposed deadlines. Often I look at how many scenes I have left to go and decide to write two per day in order to make my deadline. You could also make a daily deadline of five pages by five in the afternoon. If thinking about writing the whole rest of your story overwhelms you, see if focusing on a daily quota by a certain hour lightens you up and speeds you along.

When you make a schedule that leads to your deadline, you'll know in advance that some days will be less productive. Days that need to include special events (weddings, graduations, parties, doctor appointments) will probably be days when it will be harder to write ten pages. Plan for these days in your schedule, and then, if you do manage to write ten pages that day, you'll be ahead of the game. If you don't, you won't be behind. I always give myself a break on days when I know I'll be going on an airport run, entertaining guests, going to the dentist, taking the dog in for shots, and so on.

Another simple way to help you stick to a self-imposed deadline is to tell someone when you're going to be done. Be bold. Make a statement. "I'm going to finish my first draft by Saint Patrick's Day," you tell your brother. You are a powerful being. Your word has integrity. Words become things. You believe yourself and so your brother believes you, too. And you do finish by March 17. Because you said you would. If the person you tell doesn't believe you, you'll show them.

Recommended Reading

- *The Game of Life and How to Play It* by Florence Scovel Shinn: Advice for structuring your writing and your life.

- *The Secret* by Rhonda Byrne: Offers advice on creative visualization, positive thinking, and acts of faith.

WRITERS SUPPORT

The writing life can be lonely. You spend hours alone every week for months as you complete your novel. It's important to keep yourself connected to people and the world outside. Having a support system is important.

• **Have someone to call.** When you plan to write three scenes before dinner, call your best friend, your sister, your jogging buddy, and state your goal. Choose someone to be your support partner who believes you can write that many pages in one day, who thinks that you writing a novel is a good idea, someone who understands the true magic and power of her emotional and spiritual support of your day's work. Call that person again at the end of the day. Tell her how many pages or scenes you wrote, even if you didn't get as much done as you wanted to. There are days when this simple task makes a great difference. You write more, and better, knowing there someone is waiting to celebrate your success with you. When you do well, your support buddy validates you as a writer. And when you don't meet your goal, your support buddy still validates you. You are still a writer, even when you are not writing. All the great writers have bad days. You make a new goal for the next day and you meet your goal because you said you would. And because you're not alone.

• **Have somewhere to get away.** Removing yourself from your daily environment can help speed you through the end of your first draft. Get away to the library for two hours or rent a cabin at the beach for two days. Sometimes members of my writers support group take turns writing at each other's houses for a few hours a day for a few days in a row. We call it a writing marathon. We each find a different surface to write on (the kitchen table, the dining room table, a desk, a card table) and we don't talk—only write—from nine A.M. to noon, and after lunching together, we are quiet again from two P.M. to dinnertime. It's not only amazingly productive to be away from your phone and e-mail and pets and pile of filing for a whole day, there is a power in knowing you're not the only one producing pages of fiction in that space. You are a band of writers—adding your light together compounds the brilliance.

- **Do a coffee debrief.** When I was about to turn in the first draft of my second novel, I got a much-needed rest and a dose of inspiration by meeting my sister and a writer friend at a local bookstore for coffee. While taking a breather surrounded by literature, we shared our writing "secrets" and laughed and simply enjoyed being away from our manuscripts for a while. (My sister was rewriting a play, and our friend was deep into the first draft of a new comic novel.) By the time I got home I was recharged and ready to face a new scene. It was better than a nap, better than a Coke or chocolate, even better than a soak in a bubble bath. Make time to chat with other writers, especially when you're on a deadline and don't think you have the time for it.

- **Join (or create) a writers support group.** You could join a writers support group. Or create your own. Mine meets monthly for about three hours. There are seven of us, and we take turns cooking dinner, reporting on last month's goals, making new monthly goals, sharing heartaches and frustrations, celebrating victories, exchanging writing tips, recommending books, and giving each other emotional and spiritual support. (We also spend a lot of time laughing and talking about our lives in general.) My sister, who created the group, chose women who were already friends and whom she knew needed some support or they would not get their writing done.

• **Join (or create) a writers critique group.** In these groups you bring in samples of your writing and have the group read and give you feedback. Of course, you must also read and give feedback to the other members. Make sure this will not be too time-consuming for your writing routine. Critique groups can be great if the writers involved are good writers as well as good critics. They need to give constructive criticism, not wear you down or try to rewrite your manuscript themselves. If you're like me, you don't work well with people reading your manuscript before a rough draft is complete. But several writers I know get excellent support from their critique group members as they submit work scene by scene. There are on-line critique groups as well—explore the Internet if you think this system of support might be your thing. But be careful. If having others give you feedback starts to drain your energy, stop. Your critique group should energize you, inspire you, bring you joy. If you are feeling ground down, if you feel less like writing after your critique group meeting, move on. If you're thinking of forming a new critique group, for a good fit find people who are not only good writers but also like the same kinds of movies and books that you do. It's a good sign that they'll be open to the kind of book you're writing.

INSPIRATION

What refills your water jug best and fastest? For me, it's important to know how to quickly inspire myself. If you don't already have some tricks up your sleeve for when you're feeling an emotional slump, try a little magic.

Some things that help me when I need a shot of enthusiasm in my writing life, especially when I've been working hard for days without a break, come from my magic, or quantum physics, bag of tricks.

When I had finished *A Certain Slant of Light* and had signed with my wonderful agent, Ann Rittenberg, but didn't have a book deal yet, I decided to make an act of faith. I looked up photographers on the Internet and called a local one asking for an appointment for a publicity portrait for my book jacket. He said, "How soon do you need it?" I told him I didn't have a deadline because I didn't actually have a book deal yet, and I could tell he thought I was a bit silly, but I didn't care. It was January. I asked, "Do you have any openings in May?" He laughed and penciled me in. When I showed up in May he asked how it was going. When I told him that I'd sold my novel to Houghton Mifflin, his surprise amused me. But I wasn't surprised. I had faith. It seems to me that preparing for something does in fact call it to you faster. For inspiration, to make yourself feel happy in advance and therefore more revved up to write a great first draft, try one of these exercises.

• **Buy a "signing pen."** Buy a special pen and set it aside. Later you'll take it to a book signing. This worked for me. I bought my fancy "signing pen" in 2002 and used it at the Pacific Northwest Booksellers Association convention three years later.

- **Pack for a book tour.** After I had a book deal, but before the book was out, I bought a purse and stocked it with gum, tissues, mints, sunglasses, and a pen. Then I left it sitting out and told myself, "I will not put this purse away until my publishers fly me out to theEast Coast to meet my editor." And I did leave it out. It stayed on display for a year until I was sent to Book Expo in New York where I got to meet my editor and agent in person for the first time. So get your overnight case stocked with a book of crossword puzzles, a granola bar, and a bottle of vitamins. Be ready.

- **Have the champagne chilled.** While you're waiting to sign with an agent or land your first book deal, keep at least a miniature bottle of champagne in the door of the fridge. As soon as you get that phone call, you want to be able to have a toast with your spouse, children, or roommate. Stocking it in advance means you're ready for success.

- **Write down your perfect day.** Every morning write down how you want the day to go. Don't say, "I hope I get good news." State it as if it is a certainty. "I will get great news from my agent. The weather will be beautiful. I'll get a check in the mail." Even if everything in your vision doesn't happen that day, creating it on paper puts you in a positive state of mind. (Make sure you say the positive version of each statement. Not, "I won't get writer's block." Rather, "I'll get lots of wonderful writing done.")

- **Do daily visioning.** Sit down after breakfast in the morning and spend five minutes with your eyes closed envisioning something positive—signing with that agent, getting a rave review from your critique group, having the movie of your novel filmed with your favorite star in the lead, being twenty pounds lighter, having a joyous wedding day. Whatever you want today, next month, next year. Whatever you want your life to be like. Picture it and feel the happiness it brings you. It's even more powerful if you can do this with another person. Take turns envisioning each other's dreams. Tell each other what you saw during those five minutes of quiet meditation. For three mornings in a row, my sister and I focused on a foreign sale for my first novel that would be large enough to assist me with the fees for adopting a baby. By the fourth day I found out there had been an auction for the German rights and that they had sold for 20,000 euros. This was over three times more than any of my previous foreign deals. And it was more than enough to pay for the adoption. This felt as if it proved that what you envision does not need to be logical. It needs to feel good to you. What makes you feel joy all through your body, mind, heart, soul? Concentrate on that bliss in a state of meditation five minutes a day. See what happens.

- **Wear something that makes you feel like a rich writer.** Inspire yourself to write a moneymaker by feeling wealthy. I often wear pling-pling (play bling-bling: fake gems, etc.) while I work on my novels because it reminds that these books will not only be good, they'll make me (and my agent and publisher) lots of money. The faux diamond ring feels heavy and glamorous on my hand. See what makes you feel wealthy.

- **Count your blessings**. One way to bring success to you is to be grateful for the things you have already. You want the second half of your novel to come out as good as the first? Thank the universe for those opening chapters. You want a second book deal? Give thanks for the first and your career so far. You want to make enough money to buy a house? Be grateful for the apartment you have now. Make a list. Bless all that you have and feel the joy of each thing—your talent, your agent, your support group, your family, your friends, your new idea. The more you are grateful for, the more things to be grateful for you will draw to yourself.

- **E-mail yourself.** My friend Marc Acito told me that when he was waiting for good news from his editor or agent he would write himself an e-mail, as if he were that editor or agent, and put in it all the great news and praise for his work that he hoped to get soon. He'd e-mail it to himself, wait a while, then open his e-mail and read it, feeling the joy of having received the real thing. I tried this technique and it does feel good. Soon after I wrote an e-mail to myself as if it were from my editor, I got an e-mail from her with two of the phrases I had made up repeated almost exactly. (Just make sure you don't type your editor's address in by mistake and send it to her. That could be really embarrassing.)

- **Tear down the wall.** As a positive visualization exercise before my first novel sold, I used to meditate on a certain scene. It was different every time, but certain things were always the same. I always saw the wall between me and being a published novelist as a tall stone wall, and I always saw myself breaking through it. Sometimes I came at it with a hammer, sometimes a battering ram. Sometimes I was alone, sometimes with a whole crowd of friends and family. Once I even pictured myself standing in front of the wall and singing a big note that made the wall crumble like a trumpet blast bringing down the walls of Jericho. And I always pictured myself crossing to the other side of the wall and celebrating with my comrades in the garden that lay beyond. Eventually I started imaging that I took the stones from the broken wall and made nice things out of them in my garden of success: a flower bed wall, a bench, a bird bath. And I began to imagine that the garden was full of trees, flowers, and bushes carved in topiary sculpture that each represented a successful book I would get published one day. I don't know exactly how this works or why, but it felt like it helped me. Try it. It couldn't hurt. Imagine your success, whatever the next step looks like, as a beautiful place very close by and the barriers between you and that success as a wall, then smash that sucker flat.

• **Buy your domain name.** Soon you'll have fans who want to look you up on the Web. Nail down your domain name now so that when your book comes out, you'll be ready to create a Web site your fans can visit to see where you'll be doing readings and signings, to send you fan mail, and to read up on your next project.

• **Plan your party.** Make a list of who to invite, what to serve, and how to decorate for your celebration party when you sell your first (or next) novel. Draft the invitation. Get the addresses (or phone numbers) of your guests ready. The universe loves a party.

FINISHING THE DRAFT

When you're trying to finish the first draft of your novel and you are nearing the end, sometimes doubt will rise up and try to slow you down. If you feel something dragging at your energy as you approach the climax of your story, you may be subconsciously worrying about the quality of the book. You wonder if you're just fooling yourself. You feel as if what started out as a hot idea has become weak and undeserving.

Everybody has moments of feeling unsure. To keep you flowing through to the finish line, here are some things that might help:

- **A great opening.** Go back and read your opening page. It's wonderful. You feel inspired and off you go. Or it's less than wonderful. Take an hour and rework it. *Now* it's wonderful!

- **A great ending.** Unless you're one of those writers who literally does not know how the novel will end until you write the last line, write the ending before you get there and rewrite it when you really do get there. Or if you'd rather not write it ahead of time, at least picture it, all the cool details, the touching or shocking or clever last line that will do justice to the story. Knowing you have a worthy final page will help carry you through to the end of the draft.

- **Moments in place.** The same goes for your big moments. Go back and reread them. Relish their power. Imagine two fans discussing these moments at a book club. Imagine the movie producers who will option your book talking about how best to do justice to these amazing scenes. And if you don't feel good enough about your moments, take an hour and punch them up. Knowing that you have a great opening, a wonderful ending, and terrific moments will give you an amazing boost of energy when you need one.

- **Skip around.** When I'm trying to get through a draft quickly without sacrificing quality, I sometimes skip around and write whichever scene feels the most piping hot and ready to be written. I have a list of all the scenes and "bits" (pieces of summary or reflection) that still have to be written, and I go first to the ones to which I feel the strongest draw.

- **Skip ahead.** When I'm sprinting along and I get stalled by something small, I write that missing tidbit in caps, INSERT RESTAURANT NAME HERE or PUT IN RIGHT KIND OF TAXI, and I come back to it later. It isn't an important enough point to slow me down in my finishing of the draft, but I want to make sure I notice what I've skipped. The caps help reassure me that I'll see these gaps later, but for now I can fly ahead.

- **Skip transitions.** Something that also helps me zoom along, if I already have the opening, the ending, and the best moments written, is to not worry about writing transitions until after I've completed the first rough draft. I write my scenes using the "Shortcuts to the Scene" exercise (see chapter four) and then just move to the next scene. As I mentioned above about skipping around, I type TRANS where I'll need to later insert the transition between one scene and another or between a "bit" of summary or reflection and a scene, so I can see where I have to go back.

- **Switch gears.** If you feel stuck as you near the end of your draft, don't force yourself to crank out writing that you know is bad. Instead do something else, such as a bit of research for your novel, until you get unstuck about the scene that stumped you. This way you carry on with the quality and you won't have a poorly written scene to revise.

BLESSINGS TO THE HAPPY FEW

There may be times when writers are competitive with each other, when we hear of a book deal we wish were ours, when we think there's something on the *New York Times* best-seller list that we could've written better, when we read a rave book review that we covet, but for the most part we celebrate each other. Novelists need each other and love each other, because novelists are novel readers, and we need new books to read. We wish each other the best of luck because we want more *great* books to read. So get out there and write me some beautiful, funny, heartbreaking, fascinating, nail-biting, brilliant novels, my comrades. For we are a strange but loyal band of fellows, and we take care of each other.

Fun Stuff

- Make an act of faith by deciding what to wear for your publicity photo and researching photographers in town.

- Make a contact list (people to e-mail, write to, call, or fax) for when your book first becomes available for sale.

- Make a possible calendar for success (June: sign with an agent; July: get portrait done; August: sell first novel; September: meet editor and agent in person; and so on).

- Write your novel's dedication and acknowledgments in advance.

INDEX

ABOUT THE AUTHOR

Laura Whitcomb grew up in Pasadena, California, in a mildly haunted house. She received her English degree at California State University at Northridge in 1993. She has taught language arts in California and Hawaii. She has won three Kay Snow Awards and was once runner-up in the Bulwer-Lytton writing contest for the best first sentence of the worst science fiction novel never written. She is the author of the novels *A Certain Slant of Light* (2005) and *The Fetch* (2009), both for Houghton Mifflin Harcourt. She also coauthored *Your First Novel* (2006) with literary agent Ann Rittenberg for Writer's Digest Books. She lives in Portland, Oregon, with her dog, Maximus.